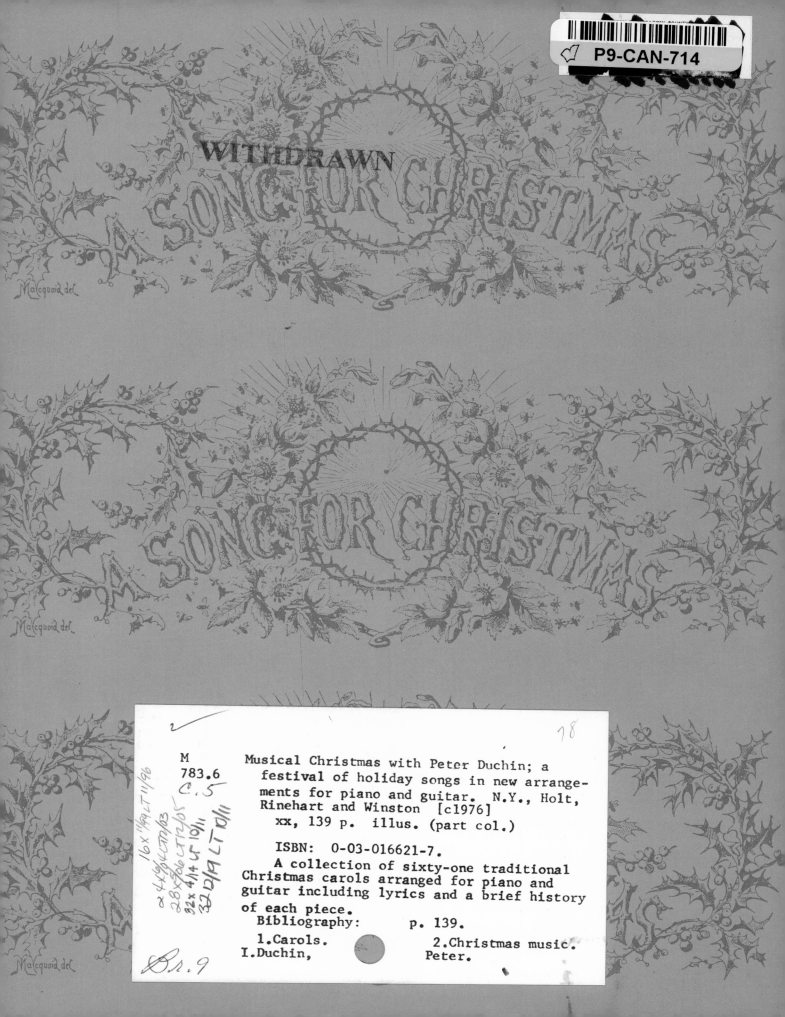

A Musical Christmas with Peter Duchin

A Musical Christmas with Peter Duchin

A FESTIVAL OF HOLIDAY SONGS IN NEW ARRANGEMENTS FOR PIANO AND GUITAR

HOLT, RINEHART AND WINSTON · NEW YORK

Front cover and title page illustration:
Copyright © 1976 by James Wyeth.

Back cover illustration: *Old Kris* by N. C. Wyeth (1882–1945),
from a private collection, photograph courtesy of
the Brandywine River Museum.

Illustrations courtesy of The Bettmann Archive, Inc.,
pages viii, xiv, xvi–xvii, 2, 3, 9, 25, 43, 49, 60,
79, 91, 103, 105, 109, 119.
Illustrations courtesy of The New York Public Library Picture Collection,
pages i, 7, 36, 39, 41, 47, 51, 53, 55, 59, 61, 65, 69, 71,
75, 81, 83, 89, 93, 101, 111, 113,
117, 122, 123, 133, 137, 138, 140.
Illustrations courtesy of the Dover Pictorial Archives,
endpapers and pages v, xi, xiii, 5, 11, 13, 14–15, 17,
21, 27, 31, 45, 57, 62, 63, 73, 77, 87,
120–121, 124, 125, 126, 127, 128, 129, 130, 131, 132.
Illustrations courtesy of Hallmark Cards, Inc.,
pages vi, 1, 19, 22, 33, 35, 67, 85, 95, 97, 99, 107, 115.

Visiting Santa Claus.

To my wife Cheray, also to
my children,
and of course to Malcolm

The first known Christmas card, created for Sir Henry Cole by John C. Horsley in 1843

Contents

"Santa Claus Waiting for the Children to Get to Sleep," by Thomas Nast, 1876

"Santa Claus in the Act of Descending a Chimney on Christmas Eve,"
from *The Great Pictorial Annual Brother Jonathan*, January 1, 1845

"The holiday letter from school.
A boy's dream of the coming Christmas."
After Adrien Marie, 1889

Acknowledgments

I should like to thank my good friend Jamie Wyeth for consenting to contribute to this volume. Obviously, Christmas means a great deal to him, and that he can express his feelings with such vitality and humor is a marvelous gift.

Samuel Hope and Robbie Gunstream were of invaluable assistance in the selection and arrangement of material. The Yale School of Music kindly allowed them free run of its great library.

Thanks also to Mr. Richard Jackson at the Lincoln Center Music Library, who was always thoughtful, kind, and helpful.

Introduction

Christmas when I was a young child was always snowy, crisp, unpolluted (we lived in the country), and incredibly active. We had an old, shaggy horse called "Jenny Strawberry Roan" for no apparent reason, for she was neither strawberry-colored nor a roan, and it seemed to be her destiny to pull a small wooden cart in the summertime, and a rather old yet still grand sleigh in the winter. When the snows came, Jenny's ears would perk up, her nostrils would flair, and she would give a snort or two signifying that she realized the sledding season was fast upon her. By Christmastime (it seemed to snow earlier in those days) Jenny was as happy as could be, proudly pulling her sleigh and occasionally even us young skiers, desperately clutching frayed ropes trailing from her harness as she cantered down snowy lanes. On Christmas Day, we always went to church—a small country church —where the minister, a kind man with the improbable name of Dr. Dumbell (he was anything but) would in a croaking yet firm voice lead us in the singing of many, many Christmas songs. During the lesson (St. Luke, of course) we would always gape with awe at the crèche (a modest crèche, for it was wartime) and finally rush home to organize and play with the presents that we had opened just this side of dawn.

When my father returned from the war, and we got to know each other again, he made a point to sit with me every Christmas Eve and Christmas Day and play carols and other Christmas music. There I'd be, rather scared and naturally fear- ful of making mistakes, and there he'd be, trying desperately to make me feel comfortable. After a bit, I'd feel at ease and we would play through all the Christmas music we could find in the house, most of it in an old hymnbook.

My father loved Christmas music, and he especially enjoyed improvising on the choral arrangements which he found in the hymnbook. These simple improvisations taught me some very important things about music, indeed about any of the arts, though I was totally unaware of it at the time. One was, certainly, that the music of Christmas was pretty, melodic, and memorable and, more, that it could be played in many different ways. But I think much more importantly, he demonstrated by his improvisations that this music was *living* music, not music up on a pedestal, untouchable because of its religious origins and historical background. He showed it to be music from and of the people—to be played and sung joyously and openly. This lesson, I think, is one of the most important ones to learn about any art. Though much art is serious, and indeed eternal, it is also fun, joyous, and a celebration, and should, I think, be treated with the same spontaneity and honest feeling which men and women have given it through the ages. I vividly remember how my father and I played away at the piano while the family and our neighbors sang merrily in several different keys in several different harmonies but nonetheless happily, unreservedly, and above all thankfully.

Now I have my own family—my wife and young ones. I can see in my children the same near-hysterical excitement that used to grip me every Christmas Day. We still go to church, but on Christmas Eve, not Christmas Day. Our minister is not Dr. Dumbell (he's passed on), and our parish is considerably larger. But the service is still extremely beautiful (St. Luke, of course) and the crèche is well populated and ample (it's luckily not wartime). In me, the feelings of celebration and thanksgiving are there more poignant than ever. After church, we come home and sit, all of us, around the piano, to sing and play the beautiful and timeless music of Christmas. My children are nervous and edgy when I ask them to play, and it takes me a bit of time to relax them. It was on one of these Christmas Eves, realizing that the only Christmas music I had in my library was the old battered hymnbook that my father and I had used years before, that I started improvising for my children as my father had for me. I also decided to set down piano arrangements of all the songs my father and I, and now my children and I, play in the Christmas season. Thus, this book. Further, when I spoke of my intention to my good friend Bill Buckley (who, incidently, is an excellent harpsichord player), he suggested that I include as well the guitar chords for the many who play guitar and who may have trouble reading both staffs.

I had a wonderful time doing this book. It was an experience which brought back many memories. It was also an experience that involved me with a corpus of popular musical literature not only technically impressive and beautiful, but also spiritually uplifting. Christmas music is in the main a celebration of the birth of Jesus Christ—the coming of the Savior. " 'Tis the season to be jolly," goes the carol. I would add, " 'Tis the music to make the world happy."

PETER DUCHIN

I Heard the Bells on Christmas Day

Words: H. W. Longfellow · Music: John Calkin

Henry Wadsworth Longfellow wrote this poem at the height of the Civil War, in 1863, the year of the terrible, bloody campaigns at Gettysburg and Vicksburg. Completed on Christmas Day, the text contrasts the feelings inherent in war to those more traditionally associated with the Christmas story.

John Calkin was born in London in 1827 and died there in 1905. He was a prolific composer of church music and hymns, and his works enjoyed considerable popularity during his lifetime. Although some of his other music is still played, his tune used as a setting for Longfellow's "I Heard the Bells on Christmas Day" is the best known.

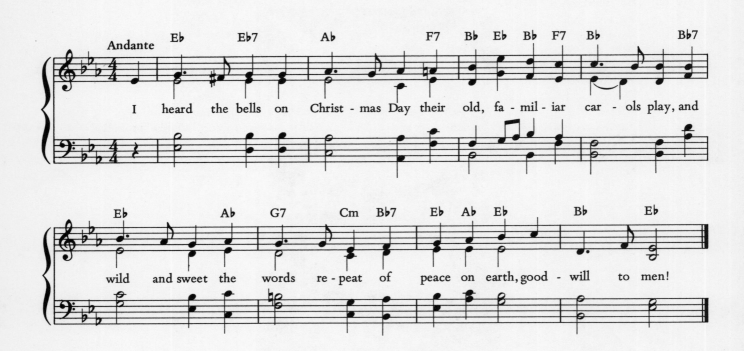

I heard the bells on Christ - mas Day their old, fa - mil - iar car - ols play, and wild and sweet the words re - peat of peace on earth, good - will to men!

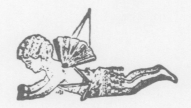

1. I heard the bells on Christmas Day
    Their old, familiar carols play,
    And wild and sweet
    The words repeat
    Of peace on earth, goodwill to men!

2. And thought how, as the day had come,
    The belfries of all Christendom
    Had rolled along
    The unbroken song
    Of peace on earth, goodwill to men!

3. Till, ringing, singing on its way,
    The world revolved from night to day,
    A voice, a chime,
    A chant sublime
    Of peace on earth, goodwill to men!

4. Then from each black, accursed mouth
    The cannon thundered in the South,
    And with the sound
    The carols drowned
    Of peace on earth, goodwill to men!

5. It was as if an earthquake rent
    The hearthstones of a continent,
    And made forlorn
    The households born
    Of peace on earth, goodwill to men!

6. And in despair I bowed my head;
    "There is no peace on earth," I said:
    "For hate is strong,
    And mocks the song
    Of peace on earth, goodwill to men!"

7. Then pealed the bells more loud and deep:
    "God is not dead; nor doth he sleep!
    The Wrong shall fail,
    The Right prevail,
    With peace on earth, goodwill to men!"

Greensleeves

Words: Traditional English · Music: Traditional English

William Shakespeare noted in his plays that this tune was a favorite of his day. Sung with its secular lyrics, it has been one of the most popular of revived folk songs:

> Alas my love you do me wrong
> To cast me out discourteously
> When I have lovèd you so long
> Delighting in thy company,
> Greensleeves is my delight,
> Greensleeves is all my joy,
> Greensleeves is my heart of gold
> And who but my lady Greensleeves.

The Christmas version's simple and charming lullaby text, generally dated 1642, has been set to other tunes, but none so popular as Greensleeves. Still another set of Christmas lyrics was composed to the melody by H. C. Dix:

> What child is this who, laid to rest,
> On Mary's lap is sleeping,
> Whom angels greet with anthems sweet,
> While shepherds watch are keeping?
> This, this is Christ the King;
> Whom shepherds guard and angels sing:
> Haste, haste to bring Him laud,
> The Babe, the Son of Mary.

Greensleeves has of course been orchestrated and reorchestrated, and I have even heard it played as a jazz tune. It is a beautiful melody, one which lends itself naturally to the flute or recorder.

Lento

The old year now a - way is fled, the new year it is en - ter - èd; then let us now our sins down-tread, and

4

joy-ful-ly all ap - pear: _____ Let's mer - ry be this day, and

let us now both sport and play: Hang grief, cast care a - way! God

send you a Hap - py New Year! _____

Fine

1. The old year now away is fled,
   The new year it is enterèd;
   Then let us now our sins down-tread,
   And joyfully all appear:
   Let's merry be this day,
   And let us now both sport and play:
   Hang grief, cast care away!
   God send you a Happy New Year!

2. The name day now of Christ we keep,
   Who for our sins did often weep;
   His hands and feet were wounded deep,
   And his blessed side with a spear;
   His head they crowned with thorn,
   And at him they did laugh and scorn,
   Who for our good was born;
   God send us a Happy New Year!

3. And now with New Year's gifts each friend
   Unto each other they do send:
   God grant we may all our lives amend,
   And that the truth may appear.
   Now, like the snake, your skin
   Cast off, of evil thoughts and sin,
   And so the year begin:
   God send us a Happy New Year!

5

We Three Kings

Words: John Henry Hopkins · Music: John Henry Hopkins

This carol was written by an American minister, J. H. Hopkins. It tells the story of the Three Wise Men or Kings, as found in St. Matthew, the first book of the New Testament. Upon seeing a star which announced to them the birth of the King of the Jews, the Three Kings—who by the Middle Ages had taken on the names of Melchior, Casper, and Balthazar—set out with gifts.

Hearing of their quest, King Herod detained them to ask that they report to him once they had found the prophesied child. The Three Wise Men followed the star which "went before them until it came and stood over where the child was." They adored the child and offered him their now-famous gifts of gold, frankincense (a sweet-smelling incense), and myrrh (a resin out of which incense is made). "And having received an answer in sleep that they should not return to Herod, they went back another way into their country." Herod then flew into a rage and killed all the male children of two years or less in Bethlehem. Joseph, however, having been warned by an angel in his sleep, had taken the baby and its mother to Egypt.

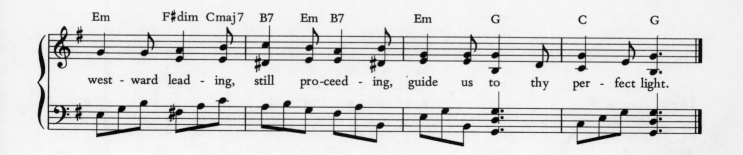

west - ward lead - ing, still pro-ceed - ing, guide us to thy per - fect light.

1. We three kings of Orient are,
   Bearing gifts we traverse afar,
   Field and fountain, moor and mountain,
   Following yonder star.

   Refrain:
   O, star of wonder, star of night,
   Star with royal beauty bright,
   Westward leading, still proceeding,
   Guide us to they perfect light.

2. Born a King on Bethlehem's plain,
   Gold I bring to crown him again
   King forever, ceasing never,
   Over us all to reign.

3. Frankincense to offer have I,
   Incense owns a Deity nigh;
   Prayer and praising, all men raising,
   Worship him, God on high.

4. Myrrh is mine: its bitter perfume
   Breathes a life of gathering gloom;
   Sorrowing, sighing, bleeding, dying,
   Sealed in the stone-cold tomb.

5. Glorious now behold him arise,
   King and God and Sacrifice,
   Alleluia, Alleluia!
   Peals through the earth and skies.

It Came upon the Midnight Clear

Words: Edmund H. Sears · Music: Richard S. Willis

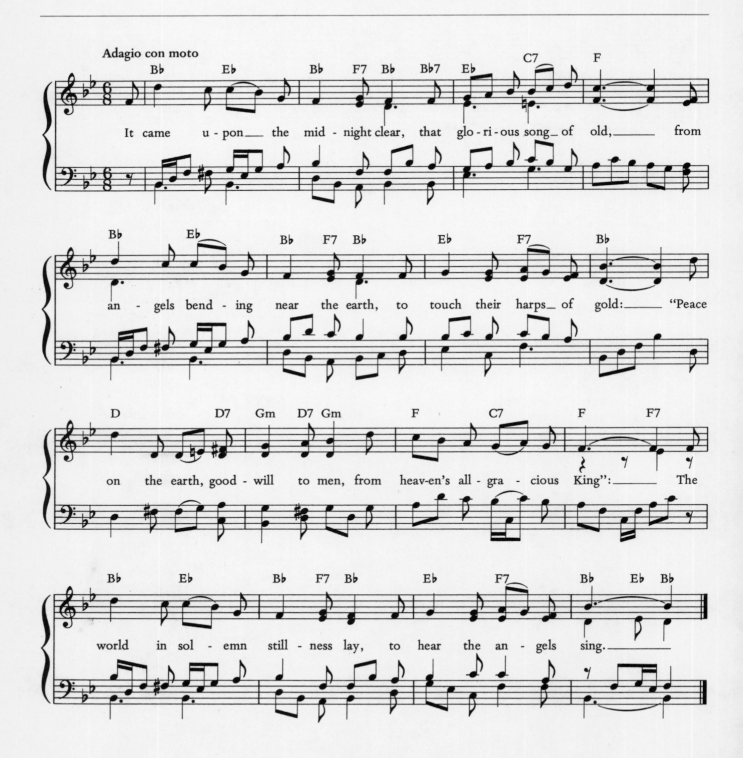

1. It came upon the midnight clear,
   That glorious song of old,
   From angels bending near the earth,
   To touch their harps of gold:
   "Peace on the earth, goodwill to men,
   From heaven's all-gracious King":
   The world in solemn stillness lay,
   To hear the angels sing.

2. Still through the cloven skies they come,
   With peaceful wings unfurled,
   And still their heavenly music floats
   O'er all the weary world:
   Above its sad and lowly plains
   They bend on hovering wing,
   And ever o'er its Babel sounds
   The blessed angels sing.

3. And ye, beneath life's crushing load,
   Whose forms are bending low,
   Who toil along the climbing way
   With painful steps and slow,
   Look now! for glad and golden hours
   Come swiftly on the wing:
   O rest beside the weary road,
   And hear the angels sing.

4. For lo, the days are hastening on,
   By prophet bards foretold,
   When with the ever-circling years
   Comes round the age of gold;
   When peace shall over all the earth
   Its ancient splendors fling,
   And the whole world give back the song
   Which now the angels sing.

Fum, Fum, Fum

Words: *Traditional Spanish, Translated by Alice Firgau* · Music: *Catalan Carol*

On December five and twenty,
Fum, fum, fum,
On December five and twenty,
Fum, fum, fum,
In a stable dark and drear was born a holy child so dear.
Born of Mary, Virgin Mother,
God's own Son who is our brother,
Fum, fum, fum.

En diciembre veinticinco,
Fum, fum, fum,
En diciembre veinticinco,
Fum, fum, fum,
Ha nacido un niñito, rosadito y blanquito,
Hijo de la Virgen pura,
Que ha nacido en un establo,
Fum, fum, fum.

As I Sat on a Sunny Bank

Words: Old English · Music: Old English

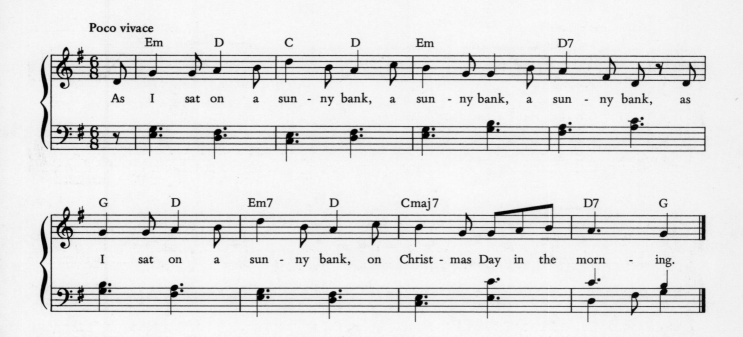

1. As I sat on a sunny bank,
   A sunny bank, a sunny bank,
   As I sat on a sunny bank,
   On Christmas Day in the morning.

2. I spied three ships come sailing by,
   Come sailing by, come sailing by,
   I spied three ships come sailing by,
   On Christmas Day in the morning.

3. And who should be with these three ships,
   With these three ships, with these three ships,
   And who should be with these three ships,
   But Joseph and his fair lady.

4. Oh, he did whistle and she did sing,
   And all the bells on earth did ring
   For joy, that our Savior He was born
   On Christmas Day in the morning.

We Wish You a Merry Christmas

Words: Traditional English • Music: Traditional English

Vivace

We wish you a Mer-ry Christ-mas, we wish you a Mer-ry Christ-mas, we

wish you a Mer-ry Christ-mas and a Hap-py New Year! Good

tid-ings to you and all of your kin, good

tid-ings for Christ-mas and a Hap-py New Year!

"Merry Old Santa Claus,"
woodcut by Thomas Nast
from *Harper's Weekly*,
January 1, 1881

1. We wish you a Merry Christmas,
   We wish you a Merry Christmas,
   We wish you a Merry Christmas
   And a Happy New Year!

   Refrain:
   Good tidings to you and all of your kin,
   Good tidings for Christmas
   And a Happy New Year!

2. Now bring us some figgy pudding,
   Now bring us some figgy pudding,
   Now bring us some figgy pudding,
   Now bring us some here!

3. We won't go until we get some,
   We won't go until we get some,
   We won't go until we get some,
   So bring us some here!

4. We all like our figgy pudding,
   We all like our figgy pudding,
   We all like our figgy pudding,
   With all its good cheer!

5. We wish you a Merry Christmas,
   We wish you a Merry Christmas,
   We wish you a Merry Christmas
   And a Happy New Year!

A
VISIT FROM
ST. NICHOLAS.
BY
CLEMENT C. MOORE, LL. D.

With Original Cuts,
DESIGNED AND ENGRAVED BY BOYD.

New-York:
HENRY M. ONDERDONK,
10 John street.
1848.

A
PRESENT
FOR
GOOD
LITTLE BOYS
AND
GIRLS.

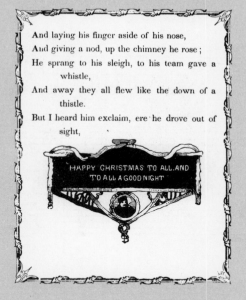

And laying his finger aside of his nose,
And giving a nod, up the chimney he rose;
He sprang to his sleigh, to his team gave a
	whistle,
And away they all flew like the down of a
	thistle.
But I heard him exclaim, ere he drove out of
	sight,

HAPPY CHRISTMAS TO ALL, AND
TO ALL A GOOD NIGHT

Title pages and illustrations from the first illustrated edition of
A Visit from St. Nicholas (The Night Before Christmas)

Christmas Eve

Words: Traditional English · Music: Traditional English

The west of England was incredibly rich in folk traditions surrounding Christmas and the Christmas season. This particular carol was an important part of such festivities. It was sung at home on Christmas Eve, and again on the festival of the nativity after the traditional eight o'clock drawing of the cakes, steaming hot, from the oven. The carol was practiced for weeks beforehand and, until the end of the eighteenth century, accompanied the consumption of the cakes, draughts of foaming ale, and mugs of cider which celebrated the occasion.

Refrain:

Now let good Chris-tians all be-gin an ho-ly life to live, and to re-joice and mer-ry be, for this is Christ-mas Eve.

---

1. The Lord at first did Adam make
   Out of the dust and clay,
   And in his nostrils breathèd life,
   E'en as the Scriptures say.
   And then in Eden's Paradise
   He placèd him to dwell,
   That he within it should remain,
   To dress and keep it well:

   Refrain:
   Now let good Christians all begin
   An holy life to live,
   And to rejoice and merry be,
   For this is Christmas Eve.

2. Now mark the goodness of the Lord
   Which He for mankind bore;
   His mercy soon He did extend,
   Lost man for to restore:
   And then, for to redeem our souls
   From death and hellish thrall,
   He said His own dear Son should be
   The Savior of us all:

3. Now for the blessings we enjoy,
   Which are from heaven above,
   Let us renounce all wickedness,
   And live in perfect love:
   Then shall we do Christ's own command,
   E'en His own written word;
   And when we die, in heaven shall
   Enjoy our living Lord:

4. And now the tide is nigh at hand,
   In which our Savior came;
   Let us rejoice and merry be
   In keeping of the same;
   Let's feed the poor and hungry souls,
   And such as do it crave;
   Then when we die, in heaven we
   Our sure reward shall have:

As Joseph Was A-Walking

Words: Old English · Music: Old English

Play with verses 1-4.

As Jo-seph was a-walk-ing, he heard an an-gel sing,___ "This night shall be___ the birth-time of Christ___ the Heav'n-ly King.___

Play with verses 5 & 6.

5. As Jo-seph was a-walk-ing, there did an an-gel sing;___ and___ Ma-ry's child___ at mid-night was born___ to be our King.___

18

1. As Joseph was a-walking,
   He heard an angel sing,
   "This night shall be the birth time
   Of Christ, The Heav'nly King.

2. "He neither shall be born
   In housen nor in hall,
   Nor in the place of Paradise,
   But in an ox's stall.

3. "He neither shall be clothed
   In purple nor in pall,
   But in the fair white linen
   That usen babies all.

4. "He neither shall be rocked
   In silver nor in gold,
   But in a wooden manger
   That resteth on the mold."

5. As Joseph was a-walking,
   There did an angel sing;
   And Mary's child at midnight
   Was born to be our King.

6. Then be ye glad, good people,
   This night of all the year.
   And light ye up your candles,
   For His star it shineth clear.

Let Our Gladness Know No End

Words: Traditional English · Music: Old Bohemian Melody

For this piece, I have made a relatively difficult piano arrangement, one which is also somewhat dissonant. I have therefore left out the chord symbols on this arrangement but inserted them over the original arrangement, which I include for those who may be daunted by my modern one.

Simple Arrangement

Let our glad-ness know no end, Hal-le-lu - jah!

Un-to earth did Christ de-scend, Hal-le-lu - jah!

Refrain

On this day God gave_____ us_____ Christ, His Son, to

save_____ us._____ Christ, His Son, His Son, to save_____ us.

1. Let our gladness know no end,
   Hallelujah!
   Unto earth did Christ descend,
   Hallelujah!

   Refrain:
   On this day God gave us Christ,
   His Son, to save us.
   Christ, His Son, His Son, to save us.

2. See the loveliest blooming rose,
   Hallelujah!
   From the branch of Jesse grows,
   Hallelujah!

3. Into flesh is made the Word,
   Hallelujah!
   'Tis our Refuge, Christ the Lord,
   Hallelujah!

CHRISTMAS.

Let holly deck the rafters and mistletoe beside,
For token of the holy time, for joy of Christmas-tide.

Harry Arnold

Carol Collecting

Most scholars agree that the word "carol" is derived from the ancient French word for round dancing, carole. The Anglo-Saxon Kyrriole may have come down from it as, later, the Chaucerian Karolle:

Upon the karolle wonder faste
I gan beholde, till atte laste
A lady gan me for to espie,
And she was clepyed Curtesie
Full curtesly she called me;
"What do you there, beau sire?" quod she
"Come, and if lyke yow
To dauncen, daunceth with us now"
And I, withoute tarrying
Wente into the Karolying.

Romaunt of the Rose

Since both the music and the words of many carols come from folk traditions that were often local and almost never written down, it is difficult to pinpoint specific origins with sure accuracy. It is believed that the popularity of Christmas carols was strengthened by the institution of a crèche in many churches, the custom being to perform circle dances with singing around the depiction of the manger scene.

In England during the nineteenth and early twentieth centuries, certain musicologists and composers became interested in collecting folk music and carols. Their aim was to record the regional words and music, taking dictation from those in the various districts of the country who were familiar with local Christmas traditions. One of the first of these collections was that of Davies Gilbert, published in 1822 under the title Some Ancient Christmas Carols with the Tunes to Which They Were Formerly Sung in the West of England. William Sandys published his Christmas Carols New and Old in 1833; he is credited with finding The First Nowell.

By the late nineteenth century the folk song movement had become nationwide and had even begun to incorporate other European folk music into the English traditions. The carol Masters in This Hall is an example. The words were written in 1860 by William Morris, who shared an office in London with Edmund Sedding, an architect and compiler of cards. Sedding was given the tune by the organist of the cathedral of Chartres in France.

Other important carol collectors were Lucy Broadwood, Cecil Sharp, Ralph Vaughan Williams, and Martin Shaw. Mrs. Broadwood took down the Sussex Mummers' Carol in the village of Horsham during the late 1870s. The renowned English composer Ralph Vaughan Williams collaborated with Martin Shaw to produce the important Oxford Book of Carols, first published in 1928. The Gloucester Wassail was collected by Vaughan Williams from an old resident of the county who sang it to him. Cecil Sharp found a similar version in the county of Somerset. The Yeoman's Carol and the delightful round, Christmas Is Coming, are of similar folk origin. The Coventry Carol and Come, Love We God, both of medieval origin, found their way into the popular repertory through the efforts of the carol collectors. The Coventry Carol was part of the Pageant of the Shearmen and Tailors, performed since the fifteenth century at the cathedral as part of the Christmas mystery or miracle plays. Come, Love We God by Richard Shann is a macaronic carol, in which the vernacular English and ecclesiastical Latin are combined. Its shifting rhythms suggest origins in the dance.

The Sussex Mummers' Carol

Words: Old English · Music: Old English

A— glo rious An- gel from Heav — en came un - to a vir - tuous

maid; strange tid - ings and great news of— joy— the hum - ble Ma - ry

1.-5. had.— The hum - ble— Ma — ry had.—

6.-7. guide.— Lord Je - sus— be his— guide.—
more and more. And give— you more and— more.— *Fine*

1. A glorious Angel from Heaven came
Unto a virtuous maid;
Strange tidings and great news of joy
The humble Mary had.
The humble Mary had.

2. O mortal man, remember well
When Christ our Lord was born;
He was crucified betwixt two thieves
And crownèd with the thorn.
And crownèd with the thorn.

3. O mortal man, remember well
When Christ died on the rood;
'Twas for our sins and wicked ways
Christ shed His precious blood.
Christ shed His precious blood.

4. O mortal man, remember well
When Christ was wrapped in clay;
He was taken to a sepulcher
Where no man ever lay.
Where no man ever lay.

5. God bless the mistress of this house
With gold chain round her breast;
Where e'er her body sleeps or wakes,
Lord send her soul to rest.
Lord send her soul to rest.

6. God bless the master of this house
With happiness beside;
Where e'er his body rides or walks,
Lord Jesus be his guide.
Lord Jesus be his guide.

7. God bless your house, your children too,
Your cattle and your store;
The Lord increase you day by day,
And give you more and more.
And give you more and more.

Christmas carol in the time of James I

Yeoman's Carol

Words: Old English · Music: Old English

Let Chris-tians all with joy-ful mirth, both young and old, both great and small,_____ now think up-on our Sav-ior's birth, who brought sal-vation to us all: This day did Christ man's soul from death re-move, with glo-rious saints to dwell__ in heav'n a-bove.

1. Let Christians all with joyful mirth,
   Both young and old, both great and small,
   Now think upon our Savior's birth,
   Who brought salvation to us all:

   Refrain:
   This day did Christ man's soul from death remove,
   With glorious saints to dwell in heav'n above.

2. No palace, but an ox's stall,
   The place of His nativity;
   This truly should instruct us all
   To learn of Him humility:

3. Then Joseph and the Virgin came
   Unto the town of Bethlehem,
   But sought in vain within the same
   For lodging to be granted them:

4. A stable harbored them, where they
   Continued till this blessed morn.
   Let us rejoice and keep the day,
   Wherein the Lord of life was born:

5. He that descended from above,
   Who for your sins has meekly died,
   Make Him the pattern of your love;
   So will your joys be sanctified:

The Gloucester Wassail

Words: Old English · Music: Old English

The word "wassail" derives from the old Anglo-Saxon drinking pledge, "Wass-Hael," which meant "Be in health." It was the custom to thus toast the lord of the manor, and the practice was easily assimilated into the Christmas tradition.

The wassail bowl is still found in England, the practice being to keep it full from Christmas Eve until Twelfth Night. In the countryside, the bowl is often carried by carolers as they offer drinks and song in exchange for alms.

Chorus
Allegretto con moto

Was-sail, Was-sail,___ all o-ver the town! Our toast it is white, and our ale___ it___ is brown, our bowl___ it___ is___ made of the white ma-ple tree; with the was-sail-ing bowl we'll drink___ to thee.

Fine

Chorus:
Wassail, Wassail, all over the town!
Our toast it is white, and our ale it is brown,
Our bowl it is made of the white maple tree;
With the wassailing bowl we'll drink to thee.

1. So here is to Cherry and to his right cheek,
   Pray God send our master a good piece of beef,
   And a good piece of beef that may we all see;
   With the wassailing bowl we'll drink to thee.

2. And here is to Dobbin and to his right eye,
   Pray God send our master a good Christmas pie,
   And a good Christmas pie that may we all see;
   With our wassailing bowl we'll drink to thee.

3. So here is to Broad May and to her broad horn,
   May God send our master a good crop of corn,
   And a good crop of corn that may we all see;
   With the wassailing bowl we'll drink to thee.

4. And here is to Fillpail and to her left ear,
   Pray God send our master a Happy New Year,
   And a Happy New Year as e'er he did see;
   With our wassailing bowl we'll drink to thee.

5. And here is to Colly and to her long tail,
   Pray God send our master he never may fail
   A bowl of strong beer; I pray you draw near,
   And our jolly wassail it's then you shall hear.

6. Come, butler, come fill us a bowl of the best,
   Then we hope that your soul in heaven may rest;
   But if you do draw us a bowl of the small,
   Then down shall go butler, bowl, and all.

7. Then here's to the maid in the lily white smock,
   Who tripped to the door and slipped back the lock!
   Who tripped to the door and pulled back the pin,
   For to let these jolly wassailers in.

Masters in This Hall

Words: William Morris · Music: Old French

Masters in this Hall, ___ hear ye news to-day ___ brought from o-ver sea, ___ and ev-er I you pray:

Refrain

No-well! No-well! No-well! No-well sing we clear! Holp-en are all folk on earth, ___ born ___ is God's son so dear:

No-well! No-well! No-well! No-well sing we loud! God to-

day hath poor folk raised___ and___ cast a-down the proud.

1. Masters in this Hall,
   Hear ye news today
   Brought from over sea,
   And ever I you pray:

   Refrain:
   Nowell! Nowell! Nowell!
   Nowell sing we clear!
   Holpen are all folk on earth,
   Born is God's son so dear:
   Nowell! Nowell! Nowell!
   Nowell sing we loud!
   God today hath poor folk raised
   And cast a-down the proud.

2. Going o'er the hills,
   Through the milk-white snow,
   Heard I ewes bleat
   While the wind did blow:

3. Shepherds many an one
   Sat among the sheep.
   No man spake more word
   Than they had been asleep:

4. Quoth I, "Fellow mine,
   Why this guise sit ye?
   Making but dull cheer,
   Shepherds though ye be?

5. "Shepherds should of right
   Leap and dance and sing.
   Thus to see ye sit,
   Is a right strange thing."

6. Quoth these fellows then,
   To Bethlem town we go,
   To see a mighty lord
   Lie in manger low."

7. "How name ye this lord,
   Shepherds?" then said I.
   "Very God," they said,
   "Come from Heaven high."

8. Then to Bethlem town
   We went two and two,
   And in a sorry place
   Heard the oxen low:

9. Therein did we see
   A sweet and goodly may
   And a fair old man.
   Upon the straw she lay:

10. And a little child
    On her arm had she.
    "Wot ye who this is?"
    Said the hinds to me:

11. Ox and ass him know,
    Kneeling on their knee.
    Wondrous joy had I
    This little babe to see:

12. This is Christ the Lord,
    Masters be ye glad!
    Christmas is come in,
    And no folk should be sad:

31

Coventry Carol

Words: Pageant of the Shearmen and Tailors, 15th Century · Music: English, 16th Century

Chorus:
Lully, lulla, thou little tiny child,
By by, lully lullay,
Thou little tiny child,
By by, lully lullay

1. O sisters too,
   How may we do
   For to preserve this day
   This poor youngling,
   For whom we do sing,
   By by, lully lullay!

2. Herod, the king,
   In his raging,
   Charged he hath this day
   His men of might,
   In his own sight,
   All young children to slay.

3. That woe is me,
   Poor child for thee!
   And ever morn and day,
   For thy parting
   Neither say nor sing
   By by, lully lullay!

Come, Love We God

Words: Richard Shann · Music: Richard Shann

1. Come, love we God! of might is most
   The Father, Son, the Holy Ghost,
   Regnante jam in aethera;[1]
   The which made man, both more and less,
   And create him to His likeness,
   O quanta, O quanta sunt haec opera.[2]

2. The herdsmen came with their off'ring
   For to present that pretty thing
   Cum summa reverentia.[3]
   They gave their gifts that child until;
   They were received with full goodwill;
   Quam grata, quam grata sunt haec munera![4]

3. Three Kinges came from the east country,
   Which knew they by astronomy,
   Et Balam vaticinia;[5]
   They offered him gold, myrrh, incense;
   He took them with great diligence:
   Quam digna, quam digna est infantia![6]

4. They turned again full merrily,
   Each came unto his own country:
   O Dei mirabilia,[7]
   They had heaven's bliss at their ending,
   The which God grant us old and young.
   Deo Patri, Deo Patri sit gloria.[8]

1. Now reigning in the sky.
2. How great are these works.
3. With utmost reverence.
4. How welcome are these gifts.
5. And by the prophecy by Balaam.
6. How worthy is the infancy.
7. O Wonderful God.
8. Glory be to God the Father.

Christmas Is Coming

Words: Unknown • Music: Old English

Allegro ma non troppo

*May be sung as a round using I, II, III as entrances.

1. Christmas is coming! The goose is getting fat!
   Please to put a penny in an old man's hat,
   Please to put a penny in an old man's hat.

2. If you've no penny, a ha'penny will do,
   If you have no ha'penny, then God bless you,
   If you have no ha'penny, then God bless you.

Away in a Manger

Words: Martin Luther   .   Music: Traditional German

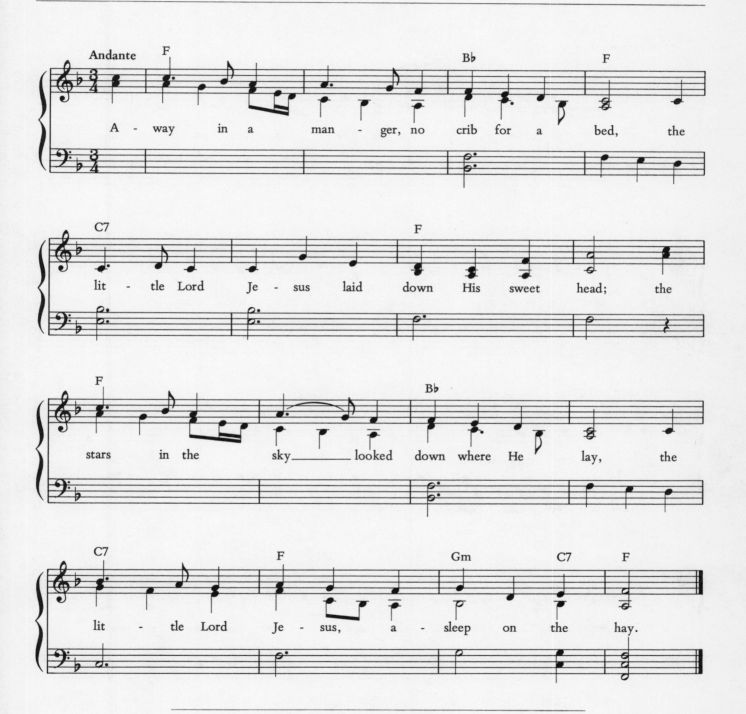

1. Away in a manger, no crib for a bed,
   The little Lord Jesus laid down His sweet head;
   The stars in the sky looked down where He lay,
   The little Lord Jesus, asleep on the hay.

2. The cattle are lowing, the poor Baby wakes,
   But little Lord Jesus, no crying He makes;
   I love Thee, Lord Jesus! look down from the sky,
   And stay by my cradle 'til morning is nigh.

O Little Town of Bethlehem

Words: Phillips Brooks · Music: Lewis Redner

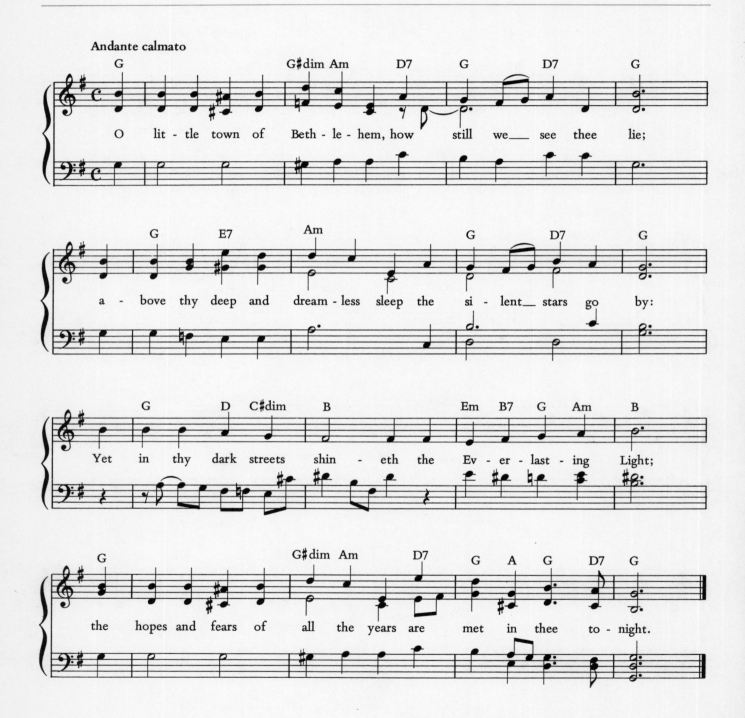

O lit - tle town of Beth - le - hem, how still we__ see thee lie;

a - bove thy deep and dream - less sleep the si - lent__ stars go by:

Yet in thy dark streets shin - eth the Ev - er - last - ing Light;

the hopes and fears of all the years are met in thee to - night.

1. O little town of Bethlehem,
   How still we see thee lie;
   Above thy deep and dreamless sleep
   The silent stars go by:
   Yet in thy dark streets shineth
   The Everlasting Light;
   The hopes and fears of all the years
   Are met in thee tonight.

2. For Christ is born of Mary,
   And gathered all above,
   While mortals sleep, the angels keep
   Their watch of wondering love.
   O morning stars, together
   Proclaim the holy birth!
   And praises sing to God the King,
   And peace to men on earth!

3. How silently, how silently
   The wonderous gift is given!
   So God imparts to human hearts
   The blessings of his heaven;
   No ear may hear his coming,
   But in this world of sin,
   Where meek souls will receive him, still
   The dear Christ enters in.

4. O holy Child of Bethlehem!
   Descend to us, we pray;
   Cast out our sin, and enter in,
   Be born in us today.
   We hear the Christmas angels
   The great glad tidings tell;
   O come to us, abide with us,
   Our Lord Emmanuel!

The First Nowell

Words: Old English · Music: Old English

Some scholars claim this carol to be French, some claim it to be English. We do know that it is one of the oldest carols in existence, and certainly one of the prettiest. Many people enjoy harmonizing the chorus, a practice that can be said to have a noble tradition, for legend has it that when shepherds in the old days sang this carol in the fields and mountains around Christmastime, the angels would join in the chorus.

The first No - well, the an - gels did say, was to cer - tain poor shep - herds, in fields as they lay, in fields where they lay a - keep - ing their sheep, on a cold win - ter's night that was so

deep. No - well,____ No - well, No - well, No -

well, born is the King____ of Is - ra - el!

1. The first Nowell, the angels did say,
   Was to certain poor shepherds, in fields as they lay,
   In fields where they lay a-keeping their sheep,
   On a cold winter's night that was so deep.

   Refrain:
   Nowell, Nowell, Nowell, Nowell,
   Born is the King of Israel!

2. They lookèd up and they saw a star
   Shining in the east beyond them far,
   And to the earth it gave great light,
   And so it continued both day and night.

3. And by the light of that same star,
   Three Wise Men came from a country afar,
   To seek for a king was their intent,
   And to follow the star wherever it went.

4. This star drew nigh to the northwest,
   O'er Bethlehem then it took its rest,
   And there it did both stop and stay,
   Right over the place where Jesus lay.

5. Then enterèd in those Wise Men three
   Full rev'rently upon their knee,
   And offered there in his presence
   Their gold and myrrh and frankincense.

Deck the Halls

Words: Old Welsh · Music: Old Welsh

This is an old Welsh Christmas song that was probably sung in the home as people decorated their trees and rooms with Christmas adornments, and as they observed the marvelous English custom of the Yule log. Every Christmas season, families (at least those with large fireplaces) would go out into the woods to cut the thickest, greenest log that they could find. Green, because the ensuing revelry would last only as long as the Yule log burned.

Troll the an-cient Yule-tide car-ol, Fa la la la la la la la la.

1. Deck the halls with boughs of holly!
   Fa la la la la la la la la.
   'Tis the season to be jolly,
   Fa la la la la la la la la.
   Don we now our gay apparel,
   Fa la la la la la la la la.
   Troll the ancient Yule-tide carol,
   Fa la la la la la la la.

2. See the blazing Yule before us,
   Fa la la la la la la la la.
   Strike the harp and join the chorus,
   Fa la la la la la la la la.
   Follow me in merry measure,
   Fa la la la la la la la la.
   While I tell of Yule-tide treasure,
   Fa la la la la la la la la.

3. Fast away the old year passes,
   Fa la la la la la la la la.
   Hail the new, ye lads and lasses,
   Fa la la la la la la la la.
   Sing we joyous all together,
   Fa la la la la la la la la.
   Heedless of the wind and weather,
   Fa la la la la la la la la.

German engraving showing
a professional salesman of
Christmas plants

Christmas Day in the Morning

Words: Old English · Music: Old English

This is a very old English carol, probably going back over five hundred years. Also known as I Saw Three Ships, it relates to an old legend that three ships (could they possibly symbolize the Wise Men?) set out to sea on the morning of Christmas Day.

Play 6 times, then go to variation below.

1. I saw three ships come sailing in,
   On Christmas Day, on Christmas Day;
   I saw three ships come sailing in,
   On Christmas Day in the morning.

2. And what was in those ships all three,
   On Christmas Day, on Christmas Day?
   And what was in those ships all three,
   On Christmas Day in the morning?

3. Our Savior Christ and his ladie,
   On Christmas Day, on Christmas Day;
   Our Savior Christ and his ladie,
   On Christmas Day in the morning.

4. Pray whither sailed those ships all three?
   On Christmas Day, on Christmas Day;
   Pray whither sailed those ships all three?
   On Christmas Day in the morning.

5. Oh, they sailed into Bethlehem,
   On Christmas Day, on Christmas Day;
   Oh, they sailed into Bethlehem,
   On Christmas Day in the morning.

6. And all the bells on earth shall ring,
   On Christmas Day, on Christmas Day;
   And all the bells on earth shall ring,
   On Christmas Day in the morning.

7. And all the angels in heav'n shall sing,
   On Christmas Day, on Christmas Day;
   And all the angels in heav'n shall sing,
   On Christmas Day in the morning.

8. And all the souls on earth shall sing,
   On Christmas Day, on Christmas Day;
   And all the souls on earth shall sing,
   On Christmas Day in the morning.

9. Then let us all rejoice amain,
   On Christmas Day, on Christmas Day;
   Then let us all rejoice amain,
   On Christmas Day in the morning.

Angels, from the Realms of Glory

Words: James Montgomery · Music: Henry Smart

1. Angels, from the realms of glory,
   Wing your flight o'er all the earth;
   Ye who sang creation's story,
   Now proclaim Messiah's birth:

   Refrain:
   Come and worship, come and worship,
   Worship Christ the newborn King.

2. Shepherds in the fields abiding,
   Watching o'er your flocks by night,
   God with man is now residing;
   Yonder shines the infant Light:

3. Sages, leave your contemplations;
   Brighter visions beam afar;
   Seek the great Desire of Nations;
   Ye have seen His natal star:

4. Saints before the altar bending,
   Watching long in hope and fear,
   Suddenly the Lord, descending,
   In His temple shall appear:

5. Though an infant now we view Him,
   He shall fill His Father's throne,
   Gather all the nations to Him;
   Every knee shall then bow down:

From "Annunciation to the Shepherds," Les Grandes Heures de Rohan, France, 1400–1450

Here We Come A-Caroling

Words: Old English · Music: Old English

This old English carol is also called **Here We Come A-Wassailing,** *referring to the old English custom of making merry and drinking "wassail" (good health) from house to house starting on Christmas Eve and continuing over the twelve days of the holiday season. It is said that many a reveler was lost in the snow, only to be found days later happily humming this carol.*

Here we come a-car-ol-ing a-mong the leaves so green,

here we come a-wan-d'ring so fair to be seen:

Refrain

Love and joy come to you, and to you your was-sail too, and God bless you, and

send you a Hap-py New Year, and God send you a Hap-py New Year.

1. Here we come a-caroling
   Among the leaves so green,
   Here we come a-wand'ring
   So fair to be seen:

   Refrain:
   Love and joy come to you,
   And to you your wassail too,
   And God bless you,
   And send you a Happy New Year,
   And God send you a Happy New Year.

2. We are not daily beggars
   That beg from door to door,
   But we are neighbors' children,
   Whom you have seen before:

3. God bless the master of this house,
   Likewise the mistress too,
   And all the little children
   That round the table go:

O Christmas Tree (O Tannenbaum)

Words: Old German · Music: Old German

The evergreen has been used as a symbol of eternal life since ancient days. Beginning with the Egyptians, Chinese, and Hebrews, and later with pagan northern Europeans, tree worship or the use of tree symbols was common to many rites. The Scandinavians used the evergreen tree during the New Year season to scare away the devil.

The modern Christmas-tree tradition comes from Germany, where the tree was an important prop in a popular medieval play about Adam and Eve. The tree was hung with apples and used as the focus of the play's action. Later, it became the custom for each home to have a "paradise" tree just inside the door of each house with candles added to symbolize Jesus Christ. This practice spread from Lutheran Germany to England during the nineteenth century and was solidified in English custom and popularized by Prince Albert, the German husband of Queen Victoria.

Andante maestoso

O Christ-mas tree! O___ Christ-mas tree! Your leaves are faith-ful ev - er! O Christ-mas tree! O___ Christ-mas tree! Your leaves are faith - ful ev - er! Not on - ly green when

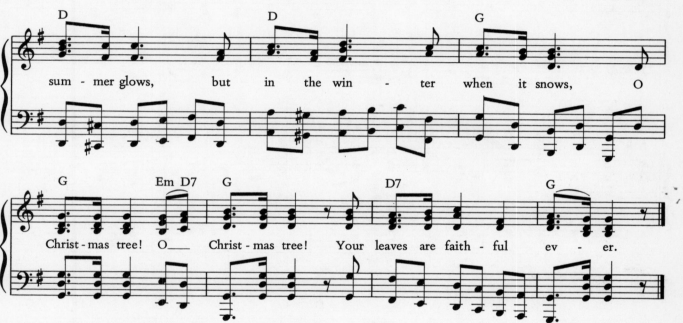

sum - mer glows, but in the win - ter when it snows, O

Christ - mas tree! O___ Christ - mas tree! Your leaves are faith - ful ev - er.

1. O Christmas tree! O Christmas tree!
Your leaves are faithful ever!
O Christmas tree! O Christmas tree!
Your leaves are faithful ever!
Not only green when summer glows,
But in the winter when it snows,
O Christmas tree! O Christmas tree!
Your leaves are faithful ever.

2. O Christmas tree! O Christmas tree!
You are the tree most lovèd;
O Christmas tree! O Christmas tree!
You are the tree most lovèd;
How oft you've given me delight
When Christmas fires were burning bright!
O Christmas tree! O Christmas tree!
You are the tree most lovèd.

3. O Christmas tree! O Christmas tree!
Your faithful leaves will teach me
O Christmas tree! O Christmas tree!
Your faithful leaves will teach me
That hope and love and constancy
Give joy and peace eternally.
O Christmas tree! O Christmas tree!
Your faithful leaves will teach me.

O Come, All Ye Faithful

Words: Latin Hymn, 18th Century · Music: Cantus Diversi, 1751

This wonderful song is perhaps as well known in Latin as in all other languages combined. Most everyone knows at least the first verse of Adeste, Fideles, yet as far as I can determine no one knows the real origin of the Latin, beyond its emergence in France as an eighteenth-century hymn. I would guess that it is more widely sung around the world than any other Christmas song.

O come, all ye faith-ful, joy-ful and tri-um-phant, O come ye, O come__ ye to Beth-le-hem! Come and be-hold Him, born the King of an-gels! O come, let us a-dore Him, O come, let us a-dore Him, O

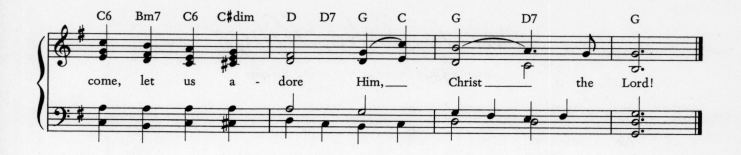

come, let us a - dore Him, _____ Christ _____ the Lord!

1. O come, all ye faithful,
   Joyful and triumphant,
   O come ye, O come ye to Bethlehem!
   Come and behold Him,
   Born the King of angels!

   Refrain:
   O come, let us adore Him,
   O come, let us adore Him,
   O come, let us adore Him,
   Christ the Lord!

2. The brightness of glory,
   Light of light eternal,
   Our lowly nature He hath not abhorred;
   Son of the Father,
   Word of God Incarnate!

3. O sing, choirs of angels,
   Sing in exultation!
   O sing, all ye citizens of heav'n above!
   Now to God be
   Glory in the highest!

4. Amen, Lord, we greet Thee,
   Born this happy morning,
   O, Jesus, forever be Thy Name adored;
   Word of the Father,
   Now in flesh appearing!

1. *Adeste, fideles*
   Laeti triumphantes,
   Venite, venite in Bethlehem;
   Natum videte,
   Regem angelorum.

   Refrain:
   Venite adoremus,
   Venite adoremus,
   Venite adoremus,
   Dominum.

2. *Deum de Deo,*
   Lumen de lumine,
   Gestant Puella viscera;
   Deum verum,
   Genitum non factum.

3. *Cantet nunc io*
   Chorus angelorum
   Cantet nunc aula coelestium.
   Gloria in
   Excelsis Deo.

4. *Ergo qui natus*
   Die hodierna,
   Jesu tibi sit Gloria;
   Patris aeterni,
   Verbum caro factum.

March of the Kings

Words: Old French · Music: Old French

Three great kings I met at early morn, with all their
were on their

ret-i-nue were slow-ly march-ing; way to meet the new-ly

born. With gifts of gold brought from far a-way, and val-iant

war-riors to guard the king-ly trea-sure, with gifts of gold brought from far a-

way, and shields all shin-ing in their bright ar - ray.

Three great kings I met at early morn,
With all their retinue were slowly marching;
Three great kings I met at early morn,
Were on their way to meet the newly born.
With gifts of gold brought from far away,
And valiant warriors to guard the kingly treasure,
With gifts of gold brought from far away,
And shields all shining in their bright array.

Provençal play
at Christmastime

Huron Carol

Words: Canadian Indian · Music: Canadian Indian

The tune of this carol is French, as adapted by a Jesuit missionary, possibly Jean de Brebeuf, who worked among the Huron Indians in Canada in the seventeenth century. He supposedly set the text, retelling the Christmas story in the Huron language, although some scholars believe that the text may have originated with the Indians themselves, for the symbolism is that of Indian lore ("Gitchi Manitou" is the Great Spirit of the Hurons). In any case, this is one of the very first and still one of the few carols to have originated in North America.

1. 'Twas in the moon of wintertime
   When all the birds had fled,
   That mighty Gitchi Manitou
   Sent angel choirs instead.
   Before their light the stars grew dim.
   And wond'ring hunters heard the hymn:

   Refrain:
   "Jesus, your King, is born.
   Jesus is born.
   In excelsis gloria!"

2. Within a lodge of broken bark
   The tender Babe was found,
   A ragged robe of rabbit skin
   Enwrapped His beauty 'round;
   And as the hunter braves drew nigh
   The angel song rang loud and high:

3. The earliest moon of wintertime
   Is not so round and fair
   As was the ring of glory on
   The helpless Infant there.
   The chiefs from far before Him knelt
   With gifts of fox and beaver pelt.

4. O children of the forest free,
   O sons of Manitou,
   The Holy Child of earth and heav'n
   Is born today for you.
   Come kneel before the radiant Boy
   Who brings you beauty, peace, and joy.

"Returning Thanks to the Great Spirit,"
a mid-nineteenth-century pictograph by Iroquois Indians

While Shepherds Watched Their Flocks

Words: Old English · Music: Old English

While shep - herds watched their flocks by night, all seat - ed on the ground, the An - gel of the Lord came down, and glo - ry shone a - round. "Fear not," said he (for might - y dread had seized their trou - bled minds); "glad tid - ings of great joy I bring to you and all man - kind."

1. While shepherds watched their flocks by night,
   All seated on the ground,
   The Angel of the Lord came down,
   And glory shone around.
   "Fear not," said he (for mighty dread
   Had seized their troubled minds);
   "Glad tidings of great joy I bring
   To you and all mankind."

2. "To you in David's town this day
   Is born of David's line
   A Savior, who is Christ the Lord;
   And this shall be the sign:
   The heavenly Babe you there shall find
   To human view displayed,
   All meanly wrapped in swathing bands,
   And in a manger laid."

3. Thus spake the Seraph: and forthwith
   Appeared a shining throng
   Of angels praising God, who thus
   Addressed their joyful song:
   "All glory be to God on high,
   And to the earth be peace;
   Goodwill henceforth from heaven to men
   Begin and never cease."

"Proclaiming the Birth of Christ to the Shepherds,"
Latin-French Book of Hours, 1514

J. S. Bach

The transcendent genius of the Baroque era, Bach was born in 1685 and over the sixty-five years of his life produced some of the most magnificent music ever written. Although he wrote in all forms, his church music is monumental. As the music director of St. Thomas Church in Leipzig for many years, he composed numerous works for the services there. His official duties called for the production of a cantata for every Sunday and feast day of the liturgical year. Of the approximately 300 he completed, only 200 survive.

Another important contribution was Bach's harmonizations of hymns or choral tunes for use in the services. The compositional skill that Bach brought to these harmonizations renders them masterpieces. The three given here have become traditional Christmas hymns. Historically, the texts of various authors have been used, depending on the country and custom, but the great music of Bach has remained unchanged.

The following three arrangements are the original arrangements of J. S. Bach. For me to depart from them seemed foolhardy, if not sacrilegious. The same considerations found me reluctant to impose guitar chord symbols over the notes. I'm confident that you will enjoy playing the unfettered, original versions.

"Music in the Home of Bach,"
engraving after the painting by Toby E. Rosenthal

Now Let All the Heavens Adore Thee

Words: Philipp Nicolai · Music: Melody from Philipp Nicolai, Harmonization by J. S. Bach

Now let all the heav'ns a - dore Thee,

and men and an - gels sing be - fore ____

Thee, with harp and cym - bal's clear - est tone;

1. Now let all the heav'ns adore Thee,
   And men and angels sing before Thee,
   With harp and cymbal's clearest tone;

2. Of one pearl each shining portal,
   Where we are with the choir immortal
   Of angels round Thy dazzling throne.

1. *Gloria sei dir gesungen*
   mit Menschen und englischen Zungen,
   mit Harfen und mit Cymbeln schon.

2. *Von zwölf Parlen sind die Pforten*
   an deiner Stadt; Wir sind Consorten
   der Engel hock um deinen Thron.

Ah, Dearest Jesus, Holy Child

Words: Martin Luther, Translated by C. Winkworth · Music: Melody from Schumann, Harmonization by J. S. Bach

Andante

Ah, dear - est Je - sus, ho - ly Child, make thee a bed, soft, un - de - filed. With - in my heart, that it may be a qui - et cham - ber kept for Thee.

1. Ah, dearest Jesus, holy Child,
   Make thee a bed, soft, undefiled.
   Within my heart, that it may be
   A quiet chamber kept for Thee.

2. My heart for very joy doth leap,
   My lips no more can silence keep;
   I, too, must sing with joyful tongue
   That sweetest ancient cradle song.

3. Glory to God in highest heav'n,
   Who unto man his Son hath given,
   While angels sing with tender mirth,
   A glad New Year to all the earth.

Watchman, Tell Us of the Night

Words: John Bowing · Music: Melody from Jakob Hintze, Harmonization by J. S. Bach

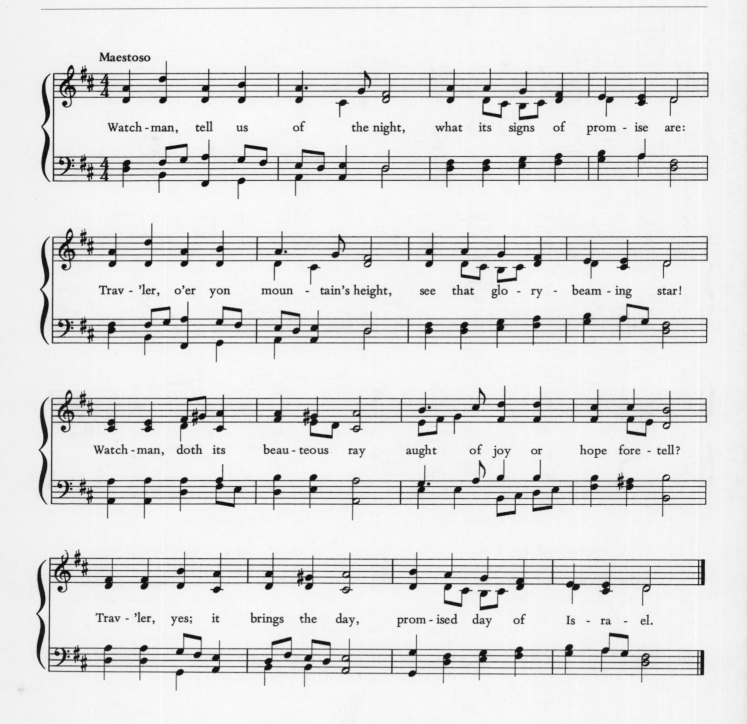

Watch-man, tell us of the night, what its signs of prom-ise are:

Trav-'ler, o'er yon moun-tain's height, see that glo-ry-beam-ing star!

Watch-man, doth its beau-teous ray aught of joy or hope fore-tell?

Trav-'ler, yes; it brings the day, prom-ised day of Is-ra-el.

1. Watchman, tell us of the night,
   What its signs of promise are:
   Trav'ler, o'er yon mountain's height,
   See that glory-beaming star!
   Watchman, doth its beauteous ray
   Aught of joy or hope foretell?
   Trav'ler, yes; it brings the day,
   Promised day of Israel.

2. Watchman, tell us of the night;
   Higher yet that star ascends:
   Trav'ler, blessedness and light,
   Peace and truth, its course portends.
   Watchman, will its beams alone
   Gild the spot that gave them birth?
   Trav'ler, ages are its own,
   And it bursts o'er all the earth!

3. Watchman, tell us of the night,
   For the morning seems to dawn:
   Trav'ler, darkness takes its flight;
   Doubt and terror are withdrawn.
   Watchman, let thy wand'ring cease;
   Hie thee to thy quiet home.
   Trav'ler, lo, the Prince of Peace,
   Lo, the Son of God, is come!

"The Youth of Bach," woodcut by Norman James

Silent Night

Words: Joseph Mohr • Music: Franz Gruber

Perhaps the most famous and familiar of all Christmas songs, Silent Night was written on Christmas Eve, 1818. Joseph Mohr, the assistant priest of the St. Nicholas Church in Obersdorf, Upper Austria, asked his organist, Franz Gruber, to set his text to music. The organ was broken, so Gruber scored the composition for two solo voices, choir, and guitar. The composition was passed about through Austria by folksingers, a distribution begun by Gruber's organ repairman. The earliest manuscript of the music is dated 1833, and it was first published in a collection of Tyrolean folk songs in 1840. Thereafter, it became world-renowned and a favorite of all ages.

Si - lent night, ho - ly night, all is calm,
all is bright round yon vir - gin mo - ther and child.
Ho - ly in - fant so ten - der and mild, sleep in heav - en - ly
peace. sleep in hea - ven - ly peace.

1. Silent night, holy night,
   All is calm, all is bright
   Round yon virgin mother and child.
   Holy infant so tender and mild,
   Sleep in heavenly peace,
   Sleep in heavenly peace.

2. Silent night, holy night,
   Shepherds quake at the sight,
   Glories stream from heaven afar,
   Heav'nly hosts sing alleluia;
   Christ, the Savior is born!
   Christ, the Savior is born!

3. Silent night, holy night,
   Son of God, love's pure light
   Radiant beams from thy holy face,
   With the dawn of redeeming grace,
   Jesus, Lord, at thy birth,
   Jesus, Lord, at thy birth.

1. *Stille Nacht, heilige Nacht!*
   Alles schläft, einsam wacht
   Nur das traute hochheilige Paar.
   Holder Knabe im lockigen Haar
   Schlaf in himmlischer Ruh,
   Schlaf in himmlischer Ruh!

2. *Stille Nacht, heilige Nacht!*
   Hirten erst kund gemacht,
   Durch der Engel Halleluja!
   Tönt es laut von fern und nah;
   Christ, der Retter, ist da!
   Christ, der Retter, ist da!

3. *Stille Nacht, heilige Nacht!*
   Gottes Sohn, O wie lacht,
   Lieb aus deinem Göttlichen Mund,
   Da uns schlägt dir rettende Stund!
   Christ in deiner Geburt!
   Christ in deiner Geburt!

He Is Born, the Divine Christ Child

Words: Traditional French · Music: Traditional French

In France, Christmas is a holiday with many traditions, one of the oldest being that of the crèche or manger. Many French homes around Christmastime put up a small replica of the manger in Bethlehem, complete with clay or wooden figures of the Christ Child, Mary, Joseph, and the Wise Men. There is usually candle-light in or near the crèche, and it is a beautiful, warm sight. These mangers with their figures are passed down through generations, so it is not unusual to see, say, a 150-year-old crèche proudly displayed in the corner of a living room, warmed by a blazing fire.

He is born, the di - vine Christ Child. Greet Him with gai - ly re - sound-ing pipe and drum.

He is born, the di - vine Christ Child. Join in song, for the Lord has come.

Proph - ets wise had fore - told His birth, pledg - ing peace to all men on earth.

Filled with hope, men be - gan to pray, till His com - ing this hap - py day.

He is born, the di - vine Christ Child. Greet Him with gai - ly re - sound - ing pipe and drum.

He is born, the di - vine Christ Child. Join in — song, for the Lord has come.

He is born, the divine Christ Child.
Greet Him with gaily resounding pipe and drum.
He is born, the divine Christ Child.
Join in song, for the Lord has come.
Prophets wise had foretold His birth,
Pledging peace to all men on earth.
Filled with hope, men began to pray,
Till His coming this happy day.
He is born, the divine Christ Child.
Greet Him with gaily resounding pipe and drum.
He is born, the divine Chist Child.
Join in song, for the Lord has come.

Il est né, le divin enfant.
Jouez, hautbois, résonnez, musettes!
Il est né, le divin enfant.
Chantons tous son avènement!
Depuis plus de quatre mille ans,
Nous le promettaient les prophètes.
Depuis plus de quartre mille ans,
Nous attendions cet heureux temps.
Il est né, le divin enfant.
Jouez, hautbois, résonnez, musettes!
Il est né, le divin enfant.
Chantons tous son avènement!

"The Adoration
of the Magi,"
French,
early fifteenth
century

Good King Wenceslas

Words: J. M. Neale · Music: Piae Cantiones, 1582

Originally a very old Bohemian "Spring" carol, this lovely song was transformed in 1853 into a Christmas carol by John Mason Neale with the addition of the verses which extol the virtues of a well-liked king named Wenceslas. The actual Wenceslas ruled Bohemia in 928–935, and little else is known about him, but from Neale's lyrics he would seem to have been not only a God-fearing, religious man, but a man who was well loved and respected by his people. The original "Spring" verses have been lost, and many scholars of hymnology still frown upon the liberties Neale took with the old song.

1. Good King Wenceslas looked out,
   On the Feast of Stephen,
   When the snow lay round about,
   Deep, and crisp, and even:
   Brightly shone the moon that night,
   Though the frost was cruel,
   When a poor man came in sight,
   Gath'ring winter fuel.

2. "Hither, page, and stand by me,
   If thou know'st it, telling,
   Yonder peasant, who is he?
   Where and what his dwelling?"
   "Sire, he lives a good league hence,
   Underneath the mountain,
   Right against the forest fence,
   By Saint Agnes' fountain."

3. "Bring me flesh, and bring me wine,
   Bring me pine logs hither:
   Thou and I will see him dine,
   When we bear them thither."
   Page and monarch, forth they went,
   Forth they went together;
   Through the rude wind's wild lament
   And the bitter weather.

4. "Sire, the night is darker now,
   And the wind blows stronger;
   Fails my heart, I know not how;
   I can go no longer."
   "Mark my footsteps, good my page;
   Tread thou in them boldly:
   Thou shalt find the winter's rage
   Freeze thy blood less coldly."

5. In his master's step he trod,
   Where the snow lay dinted;
   Heat was in the very sod
   Which the Saint had printed.
   Therefore, Christian men, be sure,
   Wealth or rank possessing,
   Ye who now will bless the poor,
   Shall yourselves find blessing.

Angels We Have Heard on High

Words: Old French · Music: Old French

The Latin hymn Gloria in Excelsis Deo ("Glory to God in the Highest") was probably the first Christmas song ever sung by a congregation. In the year 129, the Roman bishop Telesphorus ordered his people to sing this hymn as part of their religious observance of Christmas, that year and henceforth. The carol we sing here, Angels We Have Heard on High, is a small section of the original hymn.

- - - ri - a in ex - cel - sis De - o.

1. Angels we have heard on high,
   Singing sweetly through the night,
   And the mountains in reply
   Echoing their brave delight.

   Refrain:
   Gloria in excelsis Deo,
   Gloria in excelsis Deo.

2. Shepherds, why this jubilee?
   Why these songs of happy cheer?
   What great brightness did you see?
   What glad tidings did you hear?

3. Come to Bethlehem and see
   Him whose birth the angels sing;
   Come, adore on bended knee
   Christ, the Lord, the newborn King.

4. See Him in a manger laid
   Whom the angels praise above;
   Mary, Joseph, lend your aid,
   While we raise our hearts in love.

O Come, O Come, Emmanuel

Words: Latin Hymn, 12th Century · Music: Plainsong, 13th Century

This hymn is based on the early Christian liturgies. While it is apparently of non-Roman origin, its antecedents trace back to the Roman liturgy prior to the ninth century. The music derives from the seven great Antiphons (responsive chants) which were said on successive days before and after the Magnificat at vespers, from December 17 to 23, inclusive. The first English translation appeared in J. M. Neale's hymnal of 1851.

1. O come, O come, Emmanuel,
   And ransom captive Israel,
   That mourns in lonely exile here
   Until the Son of God appear.

   Refrain:
   Rejoice! Rejoice!
   Emmanuel shall come to thee,
   O Israel!

2. O come, thou Day spring, come and cheer,
   Our spirits by thine advent here;
   Disperse the gloomy clouds of night,
   And death's dark shadows put to flight.

3. O come, thou Key of David,
   And open wide our heavenly home;
   Make safe the way that leads on high,
   And close the path to misery.

Characters in Christmas play, 1873: Pharisees, Angel Gabriel, Star-bearer

Hark! the Herald Angels Sing

Words: Charles Wesley · Music: Felix Mendelssohn

For the great popularity of this rousing hymn, we can credit the fortuitous marriage of Charles Wesley's words and Felix Mendelssohn's music.

Perhaps the best-known writer of hymns and carols in the eighteenth century, Charles Wesley was the eighteenth child in a rather modest English family. He became a minister and for a time lived in colonial Georgia. Felix Mendelssohn was born in 1809 in Hamburg, Germany, into a wealthy and influential family, and died at the young age of thirty-eight, leaving a very important corpus of musical literature, both choral and instrumental.

The music for Hark! the Herald Angels Sing comes from a larger choral work that Mendelssohn had written in commemoration of the art of printing! Anticipating a text for the music, he wrote, "There must be a national and merry subject found out, something to which the soldierlike and buxom motion of the piece has some relation, and the words must express something gay and popular, as the music tries to do." His wishes were realized in 1855, when William H. Cummings added to Mendelssohn's music the words of the great Charles Wesley.

with th'an-gel-ic host pro-claim, "Christ is—born in Beth-le-hem!"

Refrain

Hark! the her-ald an-gels sing, "Glo-ry—to the new-born King!"

1. Hark! the herald angels sing,
   "Glory to the newborn King;
   Peace on earth, and mercy mild,
   God and sinners reconciled!"
   Joyful, all ye nations, rise,
   Join the triumph of the skies;
   With th'angelic host proclaim,
   "Christ is born in Bethlehem!"

   Refrain:
   Hark! the herald angels sing,
   "Glory to the newborn King!"

2. Christ, by highest heaven adored;
   Christ, the Everlasting Lord!
   Late in time behold him come,
   Offspring of the Virgin's womb:
   Veiled in flesh the Godhead see;
   Hail th'Incarnate Deity,
   Pleased as man with men to dwell,
   Jesus, our Emmanuel.

3. Mild He lays his glory by,
   Born that man no more may die,
   Born to raise the sons of earth,
   Born to give them second birth.
   Risen with healing in His wings.
   Light and life to all He brings,
   Hail the Sun of Righteousness!
   Hail the heaven-born Prince of Peace!

A Babe Lies in the Cradle

Words: German Carol, 17th Century · Music: Austrian, 17th Century

Adagio calmato

A babe _ lies in the cra - dle, a lit - tle babe _ so dear, _ with no - ble light He shin - eth as shines a mir - ror clear, _ this lit - tle babe _ so dear. _

1. A babe lies in the cradle,
   A little babe so dear,
   With noble light He shineth
   As shines a mirror clear,
   This little babe so dear.

2. The babe within the cradle
   Is Jesus Christ our Lord;
   To us all peace and amity
   At this good time afford,
   Thou Jesus Christ our Lord!

3. Who so would rock the cradle
   Where lies the gentle child,
   A lowly heart must lead him,
   By passions undefiled,
   As Mary pure and mild.

4. O Jesus, babe beloved!
   O Jesus, babe divine!
   How mighty is Thy wonderous love!
   Fill Thou this heart of mine
   With that great love of Thine.

"The Birth of Christ," Venetian woodcut

While by My Sheep

Words: Old German · Music: Old German

While by my sheep I watched at night,

glad tid-ings brought an an-gel bright. How great my

joy! Great my joy! Joy, Joy, Joy!

Joy, Joy, Joy! Praise we the Lord in heav'n on

80

1. While by my sheep I watched at night,
   Glad tidings brought an angel bright.

   Refrain:
   How great my joy! Great my joy!
   Joy, Joy, Joy! Joy, Joy, Joy!
   Praise we the Lord in heav'n on high!
   Praise we the Lord in heav'n on high!

2. There shall be born, so he did say,
   In Bethlehem a Child today;

3. There shall the Child lie in a stall,
   This Child who shall redeem us all.

4. This gift of God I'll cherish well,
   That ever joy my heart shall fill.

Painting by
Fiorenzo di Lorenzo,
Italian,
fifteenth century

As with Gladness Men of Old

Words: William C. Dix · Music: W. H. Monk

1. As with gladness men of old
   Did the guiding star behold,
   As with joy they hailed its light,
   Leading onward, beaming bright,
   So, most gracious Lord, may we
   Ever more be led to Thee.

2. As with joyful steps they sped,
   Savior, to Thy manger bed,
   There to bend the knee before Thee,
   Whom heaven and earth adore;
   So may we with willing feet
   Ever seek the mercy seat.

3. As they offered gifts most rare
   At Thy cradle rude and bare,
   So may we with holy joy,
   Pure and free from sin's alloy,
   All our costliest treasures bring,
   Christ, to Thee, our heavenly King.

4. Holy Jesus, ev'ry day
   Keep us in the narrow way;
   And when earthly things are past,
   Bring our ransomed souls at last
   Where they need no star to guide,
   Where no clouds Thy glory hide.

LA MESSE DE MINUIT

LES SOULIERS DE NOEL

LA CRÈCHE

NOEL

L'ARBRE DE NOEL

LE RÉVEILLON.

Paul Philippoteaux

God Rest Ye Merry Gentlemen

Words: Traditional English · Music: Traditional English

This eighteenth-century English carol is first found in written form in the collections known as the Roxburghe Ballads of 1770. These manuscripts are at present in the British Museum. The words are indigenous to both urban London and rural Cornwall.

Allegro marcato

God rest ye mer-ry gen-tle-men, let no-thing you dis-may, re-mem-ber Christ our Sav ior was born on Christ-mas Day; to save us all from Sa-tan's power when we were gone a-stray. O___ tid-ings of com-fort and joy, com-fort and

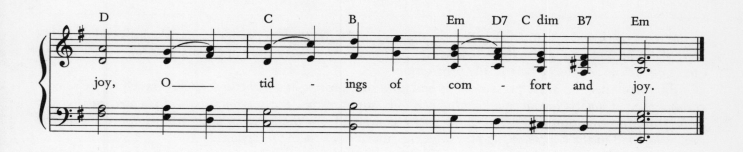

joy,   O_____   tid - ings   of   com - fort   and   joy.

1. God rest ye merry gentlemen,
Let nothing you dismay,
Remember Christ our Savior
Was born on Christmas Day;
To save us all from Satan's power
When we were gone astray.

   Refrain:
   O tidings of comfort and joy,
   Comfort and joy,
   O tidings of comfort and joy.

2. From God our heav'nly father
A blessed angel came;
And unto certain shepherds
Brought tidings of the same;
How that in Bethlehem was born
The Son of God by name.

3. "Fear not, then," said the angel,
"Let nothing you affright,
This day is born a Savior
Of a pure Virgin bright,
To free all those who trust in Him
From Satan's power and might."

4. Now to the Lord sing praises,
All you within this place,
And with true love and brotherhood
Each other now embrace;
This holy tide of Christmas
All others doth deface.

Joseph and Mary

Words: German, 15th Century · Music: German, 15th Century

In the fourteenth and fifteenth centuries, the mystery and miracle plays produced in cathedrals and churches were the principal means of religious education. At first, carols were sung in the interludes between scenes, but later the carols became part of the production.

Unfortunately, as these presentations had no written script, it is difficult for scholars to be precise concerning their dramatic arrangements. One can only suppose that the servants' parts indicated in the text came from the tradition of involving the entire community in these plays, with groups appearing in the procession and in the course of the play as representatives of their professions.

Miracle plays are still given around Christmastime in some districts and provinces of Europe, especially in Rumania and Spain. They are at times acted out by puppets, but they always incorporate the singing and dancing of old carols.

Joseph dearest, Joseph mine, help me cradle the child divine; God reward thee and all that's thine in Paradise, so

prays the moth - er Ma - ry. ry.

1. Joseph dearest, Joseph mine,
   Help me cradle the child divine;
   God reward thee and all that's thine
   In Paradise, so prays the mother Mary.

2. Gladly, dear one, lady mine,
   Help I cradle this child of thine;
   God's own light on us both shall shine
   In Paradise, as prays the mother Mary.

3. *Servant (1):*
   Peace to all that have goodwill!
   God, who heaven and earth doth fill,
   Comes to turn us away from ill,
   And lies so still within the crib of Mary.

4. *Servant (2):*
   All shall come and bow the knee;
   Wise and happy their souls shall be,
   Loving such a divinity,
   As all may see in Jesus, Son of Mary.

5. *Servant (3):*
   Now is born Emmanuel,
   Prophesied once by Ezekiel,
   Promised Mary by Gabriel
   Ah, who can tell Thy praises, Son of Mary!

6. *Servant (4):*
   Thou my lazy heart hast stirred,
   Thou, the Father's eternal Word,
   Greater than aught that ear hath heard,
   Thou tiny bird of love, Thou Son of Mary.

7. *Servant (1):*
   Sweet and lovely little one,
   Thou princely, beautiful, God's own Son,
   Without Thee all of us were undone;
   Our love is won by Thine, O Son of Mary.

8. *Servant (2):*
   Little man, and God indeed,
   Little and poor, Thou art all we need;
   We will follow where Thou dost lead,
   And we will heed our brother, born of Mary.

Bring Your Torches, Jeanette, Isabella

Words: French, 17th Century · Music: French, 17th Century

1. Bring your torches, Jeanette, Isabella,
   Bring your torches, come hurry, and run!
   It is Jesus, good folk of the village,
   Christ is born, and Mary's calling;
   Ah! Ah! Beautiful is the Mother!
   Ah! Ah! Beautiful is her Son!

2. Skies are glowing, the night is cloudless,
   Skies are glowing, come rise from your beds!
   Hasten all who would see the dear Christ Child,
   Shining and bright as yon lone star!
   Run, run! Put on your finest garments!
   Run, run! Presents for Jesus bring!

3. It is wrong, when the Baby is sleeping,
   It is wrong to cry out so loud;
   Silence, all, as you come near the stable,
   Lest your noise should waken Jesus!
   Hush, hush! Peacefully now He slumbers;
   Hush, hush! Peacefully now He sleeps.

"Adoration of the Shepherds," engraving by Jan Wierix (c. 1549–1615)

Pat-a-Pan

Words: La Mannoye · Music: Burgundian, 17th Century

Many scholars ascribe the beginning of carolry to the fusion of two forms of music, that of religious observance and that of dance celebrations. At Christmas and other church festivals, the two became combined over extended periods of time. Although the exact origin of Pat-a-Pan is vague, our best evidence is that it came into being in this fashion. The carol is a charming one, and below are its early Burgundian words:

Guil lo, pran ton tamborin,
Toi, pran tai fleute Robin;
Au son de ces instruman,
Tu-re-lu-re-lu, pa-ta-pa-ta-pan;
Au son de ces instruman,
Je dirons no ei gaiman.

1   Willie, take your little drum,
      With your whistle, Robin, come!
      When we hear the fife and drum,
      Ture-lure-lu, pata-pata-pan,
      When we hear the fife and drum,
      Christmas should be frolicsome.

2.   Thus the men of olden days
      Loved the King of kings to praise:
      When they hear the fife and drum,
      Ture-lure-lu, pata-pata-pan,
      When they hear the fife and drum,
      Sure our children won't be dumb!

3.   God and man are now become
      More at one than fife and drum.
      When you hear the fife and drum,
      Ture-lure-lu, pata-pata-pan,
      When you hear the fife and drum,
      Dance, and make the village hum!

As Lately We Watched

Words: Traditional Austrian · Music: Traditional Austrian

As late-ly we watched o'er_ our_ fields thro' the night, a

star there was seen of_ such_ glo-ri-ous light;

all thro'_ the_ night, an - gels_ did_ sing, in

car-ols so sweet of_ the_ birth of a King.

1. As lately we watched o'er our fields thro' the night,
   A star there was seen of such glorious light;
   All thro' the night, angels did sing,
   In carols so sweet of the birth of a King.

2. A King of such beauty was ne'er before seen,
   And Mary His mother so like to a queen.
   Blest be the hour, welcome the morn,
   For Christ our dear Savior on earth now is born.

3. His throne is a manger, His court is a loft,
   But troops of bright angels, in lays sweet and soft,
   Him they proclaim, our Christ by name,
   And earth, sky, and air straight are fill'd with His fame.

4. Then shepherds, be joyful, salute your liege King,
   Let hills and dales ring to the song that ye sing;
   Blest be the hour, welcome the morn,
   For Christ our dear Savior on earth now is born.

"The Three Magi Adoring the Christ Child,"
miniature from the Psalter of Queen Ingeborg, ed. 1200

Let All Mortal Flesh Keep Silence

Words: From the Liturgy of St. James · Music: Picardy Carol

This carol so reflects the traditions of its place of origin that it is known as the Picardy Carol. Its first appearance in print was in Chansons Populaires des Provinces de France, a collection published in 1860, in which it is called La Ballade de Jésus-Christ. Mme. Pierre Dupont is credited with the transcription of the music, as remembered from a song of her childhood.

Largo religioso

Let all mor-tal flesh keep___ si - lence, and with fear and trem - bling___ stand; pon-der noth-ing earth - ly___ mind - ed, for with bless - ing in His___ hand, Christ our God to earth de - scend - eth, our full hom-age to de - mand.

1. Let all mortal flesh keep silence,
   And with fear and trembling stand;
   Ponder nothing earthly minded,
   For with blessing in His hand,
   Christ our God to earth descendeth,
   Our full homage to demand.

2. King of kings, yet born of Mary,
   As of old on earth He stood,
   Lord of lords, in human vesture
   In the body and the blood,
   He will give to all the faithful
   His own self for heavenly food.

3. Rank on rank the host of heaven
   Spreads its vanguard on the way,
   As the Light of light descendeth,
   From the realms of endless day,
   That the powers of hell may vanish
   As the darkness clears away.

4. At his feet the six-winged seraph;
   Cherubim, with sleepless eye,
   Veil their faces to the presence,
   As with ceaseless voice they cry,
   Alleluia, Alleluia,
   Alleluia, Lord Most High!

All My Heart This Night Rejoices

Words: Paul Gerhardt · Music: Johann Ebeling

This hymn first appeared in print in 1653 in the Praxis Pietatis Melica of Cruger. The original text by Gerhardt was fifteen stanzas long. Catherine Winkworth made a free translation of selected stanzas for publication in her Lyra Germanica of 1861.

All my heart this night re-joic-es as I hear, far and near, sweet-est an-gel voi-ces; "Christ is born," their choirs are sing-ing till the air ev-'ry-where now with joy is ring-ing.

1. All my heart this night rejoices
   As I hear, far and near,
   Sweetest angel voices;
   "Christ is born," their choirs are singing
   Till the air ev'rywhere
   Now with joy is ringing.

2. Hark! a voice from yonder manger,
   Soft and sweet, doth entreat:
   "Flee from woe and danger!
   Brethren, come! from all doth grieve you,
   You are freed;
   All you need I will surely give you."

3. Come, then, let us hasten yonder!
   Here let all, great and small,
   Kneel in awe and wonder!
   Love him who with love is yearning!
   Hail the star that from far
   Bright with hope is burning!

Once in Royal David's City

Words: C. F. Alexander · Music: Henry J. Gauntlett

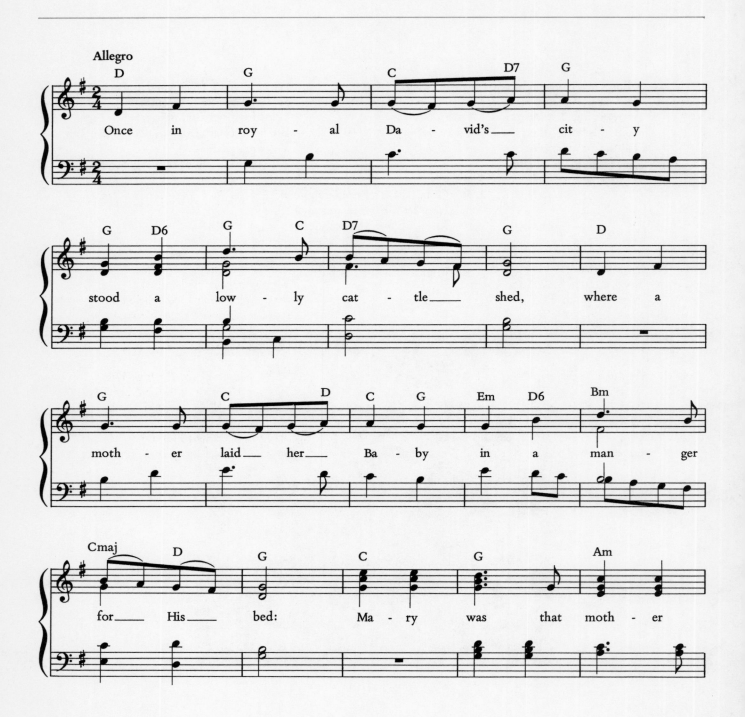

Once in roy - al Da - vid's city stood a low - ly cat - tle shed, where a moth - er laid her Ba - by in a man - ger for His bed: Ma - ry was that moth - er

mild, Je - sus Christ, her lit - tle____ Child.

1. Once in royal David's city
   Stood a lowly cattle shed,
   Where a mother laid her Baby
   In a manger for His bed:
   Mary was that mother mild,
   Jesus Christ, her little Child.

2. He came down to earth from heaven
   Who is God and Lord of all,
   And His shelter was a stable,
   And his cradle was a stall:
   With the poor, and mean, and lowly,
   Lived on earth our Savior holy.

3. Jesus is our childhood's pattern,
   Day by day like us he grew;
   He was little, weak, and helpless,
   Tears and smiles like us He knew:
   And He feeleth for our sadness,
   And He shareth in our gladness.

4. And our eyes at last shall see Him,
   Through His own redeeming love;
   For that Child so dear and gentle
   Is our Lord in heaven above,
   And He leads his children on
   To the place where He is gone.

'Twixt Gentle Ox and Ass So Gray

Words: Old French · Music: Old French

1. 'Twixt gentle ox and ass so gray,
   Sleep, sleep,
   On Thy bed of hay;
   Thousand cherubim, thousand seraphim,
   Hover high above the mighty Lord of Love.
   Sleep, sleep, sleep, King of angels, sleep!

2. 'Twixt lilies white and roses gay,
   Sleep, sleep,
   On Thy bed of hay;
   Thousand cherubim, thousand seraphim,
   Hover high above the mighty Lord of Love.
   Sleep, sleep, sleep, King of angels, sleep!

3. While Mary sings her sweetest lay,
   Sleep, sleep,
   On Thy bed of hay;
   Thousand cherubim, thousand seraphim,
   Hover high above the mighty Lord of Love.
   Sleep, sleep, sleep, King of angels, sleep!

4. On this peaceful, holy day,
   Sleep, sleep,
   On Thy bed of hay;
   Thousand cherubim, thousand seraphim,
   Hover high above the mighty Lord of Love.
   Sleep, sleep, sleep, King of angels, sleep!

"Adoration of the Magi," painting by Jerome Bosch

Christmas Eve Is Here

Words: Old French · Music: Old French

This old French carol is one of the few Christmas songs that were composed as rounds. The melody consists of sections of equal length and similar harmonic structure, allowing two or more singers, or groups of singers, to begin the song at different, regularly spaced, intervals.

Largo calmato

Christ-mas Eve is here, see, the moon is wak-ing! Christ-mas Eve is here, clear and cold the night.__ Trudg-ing thro' the snow, go the qui-et peo-ple; trudg-ing thro' the snow, go the qui-et peo-ple. Christ-mas Eve is here, clear and cold the night._____

1. Christmas Eve is here,
   See, the moon is waking!
   Christmas Eve is here,
   Clear and cold the night.
   Trudging thro' the snow,
   Go the quiet people;
   Trudging thro' the snow,
   Go the quiet people.
   Christmas Eve is here,
   Clear and cold the night.

2. People on the road
   Carry lighted lanterns;
   See their bobbing lights
   Lead the way to church.
   There they will keep watch
   Till the hour of midnight;
   There they will keep watch
   Till the hour of midnight,
   When the bells will ring
   Joyous melodies.

3. Hear the ringing bells
   Swinging far their music,
   Hear the ringing bells
   Playing merry chimes!
   Christmas Day is here,
   Day of joy and gladness;
   Christmas Day is here,
   Day of joy and gladness,
   Bringing peace on earth,
   And goodwill to men.

The Holly and the Ivy

Words: Traditional English · Music: Traditional English

In early times, when reference was made in song or verse to "holly" or "ivy," the meaning was symbolic: holly stood for the male, ivy for the female.

As was the custom in England with the old Christmas songs, this carol was printed on sheets called "broadsides" for all the people to sing.

1. The holly and the ivy,
   When they are both full grown,
   Of all the trees that are in the wood,
   The holly bears the crown:

   Refrain:
   The rising of the sun
   And the running of the deer,
   The playing of the merry organ,
   Sweet singing in the choir.

2. The holly bears a blossom,
   As white as the lily flower,
   And Mary bore sweet Jesus Christ,
   To be our sweet Savior:

3. The holly bears a berry,
   As red as any blood,
   And Mary bore sweet Jesus Christ
   To do poor sinners good:

4. The holly bears a prickle,
   As sharp as any thorn,
   And Mary bore sweet Jesus Christ
   On Christmas Day in the morn:

5. The holly bears a bark,
   As bitter as any gall,
   And Mary bore sweet Jesus Christ
   For to redeem us all:

6. The holly and the ivy,
   When they are both full grown,
   Of all the trees that are in the wood,
   The holly bears the crown:

"Moonlight in Central Park," lithograph by Haskill and Allen

The Friendly Beasts

Words: *English, 12th Century* · Music: *English, 12th Century*

This carol also seems to have origins in the medieval mystery plays.

The tune of The Friendly Beasts *was part of the Fête de l'Ane (Donkey's Festival), a celebration of the flight into Egypt that was a regular feature at Christmas observances at Beauvais, France.*

It is interesting to note that the plays took on a processional character in England, while in France they remained in a fixed stage format. As time passed, the carols grew so popular that it became a practice to sing them alone without dramatic representation.

1. Jesus our brother, kind and good,
   Was humbly born in a stable rude,
   And the friendly beasts around him stood;
   Jesus our brother, kind and good.

2. "I," said the donkey, shaggy and brown,
   "I carried His mother uphill and down;
   I carried His mother to Bethlehem town.
   I," said the donkey, shaggy and brown.

3. "I," said the cow all white and red,
   "I gave him my manger for his bed,
   I gave him my hay to pillow his head.
   I," said the cow, all white and red.

4. "I," said the sheep with curly horn,
   "I gave him my wool for his blanket warm,
   He wore my coat on Christmas morn.
   I," said the sheep with curly horn.

5. "I," said the dove from the rafters high,
   "Cooed him to sleep that he should not cry,
   We cooed him to sleep, my mate and I.
   I," said the dove from the rafters high.

6. Thus every beast by some good spell,
   In the stable dark was glad to tell
   Of the gift he gave Emmanuel,
   The gift he gave Emmanuel.

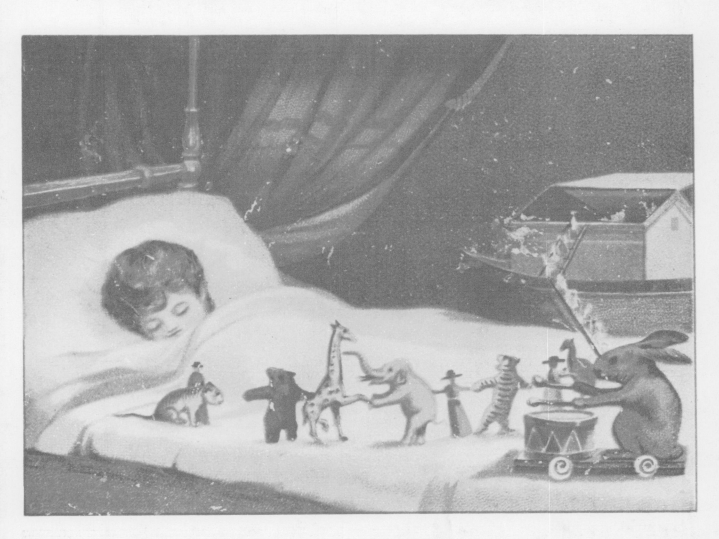

Good Christian Men, Rejoice

Words: Old German · Music: Old German

This carol is supposedly of mystical origin. A medieval text states that the words were first sung by angels to a Dominican prior named Heinrich Suso, a mystic who lived in the fourteenth century and who is said to have been drawn into a jubilant dance with the angels. The original text, In Dulci Jubilo, was macaronic— that is, words of the vernacular were mixed with Latin. A tour de force of such lingual overplay was recorded on September 14, 1745, at the Moravian Mission in Bethlehem, Pennsylvania. On that day, the mission's diary says it was sung there simultaneously in thirteen languages, including several American Indian tongues.

1. Good Christian men, rejoice
   With heart and soul and voice,
   Give ye heed to what we say:
   News! News!
   Jesus Christ is born today!
   Ox and ass before Him bow,
   And He is in the manger now;
   Christ is born today!
   Christ is born today!

2. Good Christian men, rejoice
   With heart and soul and voice,
   Now ye hear of endless bliss:
   Joy! Joy!
   Jesus Christ was born for this.
   He hath ope'd the heav'nly door,
   And man is blessed evermore;
   Christ was born for this,
   Christ was born for this.

3. Good Christian men, rejoice
   With heart and soul and voice,
   Now ye need not fear the grave:
   Peace! Peace!
   Jesus Christ was born to save.
   Calls you one and calls you all,
   To gain His everlasting hall;
   Christ was born to save,
   Christ was born to save.

Fool distributing nuts and goodies, seventeenth-century woodcut

O Come, Little Children

Words: Christoph von Schmid · Music: J. A. P. Schulz

O come, little children, O come, one and all! O come to the cradle in Bethlehem's stall! Come, look in the manger! There sleeps on the hay an Infant so love-ly, in light bright as day.

1. O come, little children, O come, one and all!
   O come to the cradle in Bethlehem's stall!
   Come, look in the manger! There sleeps on the hay
   An Infant so lovely, in light bright as day.

2. O see where He's lying, the heavenly Boy!
   Here Joseph and Mary behold Him with joy;
   The shepherds have come, and are kneeling in pray'r,
   While songs of the angels float over Him there.

3. O bow with the shepherds on low-bended knee,
   With hearts full of thanks for the Gift which you see!
   Come, lift up your voices the Child to adore!
   Sing joy to the world, love and peace evermore!

Joy to the World

Words: From Psalm 98 · Music: G. F. Handel

The text of this famous carol is a paraphrase of Psalm 98 by the great English hymn writer, Isaac Watts. The music comes from various sections of Handel's Messiah, one of the most inspired choral works ever written. The carol was compiled into its present form in 1830 by Lowell Mason, an American composer and educator.

With its contrapuntal middle section, Joy to the World is a carol that can be called truly international. Its development from a Hebrew psalm which might have been chanted in the temple of Jerusalem, to a four-square Christian hymn with German music, English translation, and American rearrangement, offers an outstanding example of the derivational quality of many of these songs.

1. Joy to the world! the Lord is come:
   Let earth receive her King;
   Let ev'ry heart prepare Him room,
   And heav'n and nature sing,
   And heav'n and nature sing,
   And heaven, and heaven and nature sing.

2. Joy to the earth! the Savior reigns:
   Let men their songs employ;
   While fields and floods, rocks, hills, and plains
   Repeat the sounding joy,
   Repeat the sounding joy,
   Repeat, repeat the sounding joy.

3. No more let sins and sorrows grow,
   Nor thorns infest the ground;
   He comes to make his blessings flow
   Far as the curse is found,
   Far as the curse is found,
   Far as, far as the curse is found.

4. He rules the world with truth and grace,
   And makes the nations prove
   The glories of His righteousness,
   And wonders of His love,
   And wonders of His love,
   And wonders, and wonders of His love.

"The Lord of Misrule," from a nineteenth-century drawing by Charles Green

Carol of the Birds

Words: *Traditional French* · Music: *Traditional French*

This carol from northern France may be another example of a song performed with animal tableaux in mystery plays. Another possible source might have been the custom of placing a sheaf of wheat atop a tall pole for the birds during Christmas season.

Whence comes this rush of wings a-far, fol-low-ing straight the No-el star?
Birds from the woods in won-drous flight Beth-le-hem seek this ho-ly night.

1. Whence comes this rush of wings afar,
   Following straight the Noel star?
   Birds from the woods in wondrous flight
   Bethlehem seek this holy night.

2. Tell us, ye birds, why come ye here,
   Into this stable poor and drear?
   "Hast'ning we seek the newborn King,
   And all our sweetest music brings."

3. Angels and shepherds, birds of the sky,
   Come where the Son of God doth lie;
   Christ on earth with man doth dwell.
   Join in the shout, "Noel, Noel!"

The Babe of Bethlehem

Words: Traditional · Music: Melody from Southern Harmony

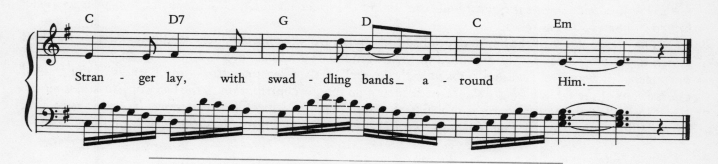

Stran - ger lay, with swad - dling bands_ a - round Him._

1. His parents poor in earthly store,
   To entertain the Stranger,
   They found no bed to lay His head,
   But in the ox's manger.
   No royal things, as used by kings,
   Were seen by those who found Him.
   But in the hay the Stranger lay,
   With swaddling bands around Him.

2. On the same night a glorious light
   To shepherds there appeared,
   Bright angels came in shining flame,
   They saw and greatly feared.
   The angels said, "Be not afraid,
   Although we much alarm you.
   We do appear good news to bear,
   As now we will inform you.

3. "The city's name is Bethlehem,
   In which God hath appointed,
   This glorious morn a Savior's born,
   For Him God anointed;
   By this you'll know, if you will go,
   To see this little Stranger,
   His lovely charms in Mary's arms,
   Both lying in a manger."

4. When this was said, straightway was made
   A glorious sound from heaven,
   Each flaming tongue an anthem sung,
   "To men a Savior's given.
   In Jesus' name, the glorious theme,
   We elevate our voices,
   At Jesus' birth be peace on earth,
   Meanwhile all heaven rejoices."

Go, Tell It on the Mountain

Words: Negro Spiritual · Music: Negro Spiritual

During early colonial days, the Puritans of New England frowned upon a festival observance of Christmas; in the English colonies of the South, however, and in the French and Dutch settlements, the event was celebrated in homes and churches.

The Negro slaves of the South developed their music from the "field holler," and from African rhythms which were, of course, deeply ingrained in their heritage. It gradually evolved into a quasi-liturgical music of tremendous power and beauty. Imbued with the spell of the Christmas story, and witness to the festival celebrations of the whites, Negro slaves made their own unique contribution to the body of Christmas music.

Go, Tell It on the Mountain is probably the most famous Negro Christmas song. Its music may have been slightly influenced by English songs, but its text is a direct outgrowth of the Negro tradition.

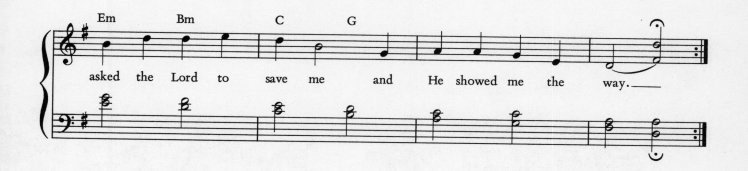

Em   Bm   C   G

asked the Lord to save me   and   He showed me the   way.____

Chorus:
Go, tell it on the mountain
Over the hills and everywhere,
Go, tell it on the mountain
That Jesus Christ is born.

1. When I was a sinner
   I prayed both night and day,
   I asked the Lord to save me
   And He showed me the way.

2. He made me a watchman
   Upon the city wall
   And if I serve Him truly,
   I am the least of all.

3. In the time of David
   Some said he was a King
   And if a child' is true born
   The Lord will hear him sing.

LVE DAYS

STMAS

The Twelve Days of Christmas

Words: Old English · Music: Old English

This carol is thought to be of French origin, intended as a song for Twelfth Night. In England it became a cumulative song for use as accompaniment to a party game of forfeits in which twelve players all contributed gifts in random order. Each player as he took his turn was required to name all the previous gifts backward, ending the series with the words, "and a partridge in a pear tree." If a participant was incorrect in the ordering of the gifts, a forfeit was demanded of him. Today the order is standardized and the song is one of the most popular secular carols.

For simple arrangement of days three through twelve, repeat from asterisk (∗) to asterisk (∗) for each new day.

122

On the first day of Christmas my true love sent to me,
 A partridge in a pear tree.

On the second day of Christmas my true love sent to me,
 Two turtle doves and a partridge in a pear tree.

On the third day of Christmas my true love sent to me,
 Three French hens, two turtle doves, and
 a partridge in a pear tree.

On the fourth day of Christmas my true love sent to me,
 Four colly birds, three French hens, two
 turtle doves, and a partridge in a pear tree.

On the fifth day of Christmas my true love sent to me,
 Five gold rings, four colly birds, three French
 hens, two turtle doves, and a partridge in a
 pear tree.

On the sixth day of Christmas my true love sent to me,
 Six geese a-laying, five gold rings, four colly
 birds, three French hens, two turtle doves,
 and a partridge in a pear tree.

On the seventh day of Christmas my true love sent to me,
 Seven swans a-swimming, six geese a-laying,
 five gold rings, four colly birds, three French
 hens, two turtle doves, and a partridge in a
 pear tree.

On the eighth day of Christmas my true love sent to me,
 Eight maids a-milking, seven swans a-swimming,

six geese a-laying, five gold rings, four colly birds,
 three French hens, two turtle doves, and a
 partridge in a pear tree.

On the ninth day of Christmas my true love sent to me,
 Nine ladies dancing, eight maids a-milking,
 seven swans a-swimming, six geese a-laying,
 five gold rings, four colly birds, three French
 hens, two turtle doves, and a partridge in a
 pear tree.

On the tenth day of Christmas my true love sent to me,
 Ten lords a-leaping, nine ladies dancing, eight
 maids a-milking, seven swans a-swimming, six
 geese a-laying, five gold rings, four colly birds,
 three French hens, two turtle doves, and a
 partridge in a pear tree.

On the eleventh day of Christmas my true love sent to me,
 Eleven drummers drumming, ten lords a-leaping,
 nine ladies dancing, eight maids a-milking, seven
 swans a-swimming, six geese a-laying, five gold
 rings, four colly birds, three French hens, two
 turtle doves, and a partridge in a pear tree.

On the twelfth day of Christmas my true love sent to me,
 Twelve pipers piping, eleven drummers drumming, ten lords a-leaping, nine ladies dancing,
 eight maids a-milking, seven swans a-swimming,
 six geese a-laying, five gold rings, four colly birds,
 three French hens, two turtle doves, and a partridge in a pear tree.

Third Day

On the third___ day of Christ - mas my true love___ sent to me,

three _____ French ____ hens, _____ two _____ tur - tle doves, ____ and a

par - tridge ____ in a ____ pear _____ tree.

Fourth Day

On the fourth day of Christ - mas my true love sent to me, four col - ly birds,

three French _ hens, two tur - tle doves, and a par - tridge _ in a pear tree.

Fifth Day

On the fifth day of Christ- mas my true love sent to me,

five gold___ rings, four___ col- ly birds, three French hens,

two___ tur- tle doves, and a par- tridge___ in a pear tree.

Sixth Day

On the sixth day of Christ- mas my true love sent to me, six geese a-lay-ing,

125

five gold___ rings, four___ col-ly birds, three French hens,

two___ tur-tle doves, and a par-tridge___ in a pear tree.

Seventh Day

On the sev-enth day of Christ-mas my true love sent to me, sev-en swans a-swim-ming

six geese a-lay-ing, five gold___ rings, four___ col-ly birds,

three French hens, two__ tur - tle doves, and a par - tridge__ in a pear tree.

Eighth Day

On the eighth day of Christ - mas my true love sent to me,

eight maids a - milk - ing, sev - en swans a - swim - ming, six geese a - lay - ing,

five gold__ rings, four__ col - ly birds, three French hens,

two— tur-tle doves, and a par-tridge— in a pear tree.

Ninth Day

On the ninth day of Christ-mas my true love sent to me,

nine la-dies danc-ing, eight maids a-milk-ing, sev-en swans a-swim-ming,

six geese a-lay-ing, five gold— rings, four— col-ly birds,

three French hens, two turtle doves, and a partridge in a pear tree.

Tenth Day

On the tenth day of Christmas my true love sent to me,

ten lords a-leaping, nine ladies dancing, eight maids a-milking,

seven swans a-swimming, six geese a-laying, five gold

rings, four___ col - ly birds, three French hens,

two___ tur - tle doves, and a par - tridge___ in a pear tree.

Eleventh Day

On the e - lev - enth day of Christ - mas my true love sent to me, e -

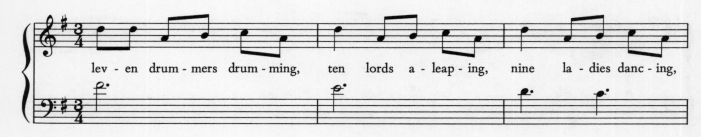

lev - en drum - mers drum - ming, ten lords a - leap - ing, nine la - dies danc - ing,

eight maids a-milk-ing, sev-en swans a-swim-ming, six geese a-lay-ing,

five gold rings, four col-ly birds, three French hens,

two tur-tle doves, and a par-tridge in a pear tree.

Twelfth Day

On the twelfth day of Christ-mas my true love sent to me, twelve pip-ers pip-ing,

eleven drummers drumming, ten lords a-leaping, nine ladies dancing,

eight maids a-milking, seven swans a-swimming, six geese a-laying,

five gold rings, four colly birds, three French hens,

two turtle doves, and a partridge in a pear tree.

rit. - - - - - - - - - - - - - - - - - - -

A rebus Christmas tree

O Holy Night

Words: Adolphe Adam • Music: Traditional

This composition by Adolphe Adam was first performed at the 1847 Christmas Eve midnight mass in the church of Roquemaure, France. In a few years its popularity had swept the land, to the dismay of some conservative church musicians who thought that its style was too nonliturgical. Nevertheless, the carol has entered the standard literature of the Christmas season, its particular mood being unique among the other Christmas hymns for its soloistic and emotional effect.

1. O ho - ly night!____ the stars are bright - ly shin - ing, it is the night of our dear Sav - ior's birth. Long lay the
2. Led by the light____ of faith se - rene - ly beam - ing, with glow - ing hearts by His cra - dle we stand. So, led by
3. Tru - ly He taught____ us to love____ one an - oth - er; His law is love and His gos - pel is peace. Chains shall He

world_____ in sin and er - ror pin - ing, till He ap -
light_____ of a star_____ sweet - ly gleam - ing, here come the
break,_____ for the slave_____ is our broth - er, and in His

pear'd and the soul felt its worth.
wise men from the Or - ient land.
name all op - pres - sion shall cease.

A
The
Sweet

thrill of hope the wea - ry world re - joic - es for
King of kings lay thus in low - ly man - ger, in
hymns of joy in grate - ful chor - us raise we, let

yon - der breaks a new and glo - rious morn._____
all our trials born to_____ be our friend._____
all with - in us praise his ho - ly name._____

night | di - vine,_____ | O_____
hold | your | King,_____ | your_____
pow'r | and | glo - - ry_____

night, | O_____ night di - vine.
King, | be - fore Him bend.
ev - er - more pro - - - - claim.

1.-2. | 3.

rit.

WHAT SWEETER
MUSIC
CAN WE BRING

THAN A
CAROL
FOR TO SING,

THE BIRTH
OF
THIS OUR

HEAVENLY

KING:

T. Pym

Bibliography

Information incorporated into my notes on many of the songs was found in several of the publications listed below. The entire listing is offered for further background on the lyrics and music of traditional Christmas songs.

Brice, Douglas. *The Folk-Carol of England.* London: Herbert Jenkins, Ltd., 1967.

Brown, Theron, and Hezekiah Butterworth. *The Story of the Hymns and Tunes.* New York: George H. Doran, 1906 (modern reprint by Scholarly Press).

Duncan, Edmondstoune. *The Story of the Carol.* London: W. Scott Publishing Co. 1911; Detroit: reissued by Singing Tree Press, 1968.

Frost, Maurice, editor. *Historical Companion to Hymns Ancient and Modern.* London: William Clowes and Son, Ltd., 1962.

Fuld, James J. *The Book of World-Famous Music.* New York: Crown Publishers, 1971.

Hutton, Edna Rait. *Carols of the Ages; Our Heritage in the Christmas Carol.* St. Louis: The Bethany Press, 1943.

Julian, John. *A Dictionary of Hymnology.* 2 vols. New York: Dover Publications, 1957 (reprint of the 2nd rev. ed., London: J. Murray, 1907).

Phillips, William. *Carols; Their Origin, Music, and Connection With Mystery Plays.* Westport, Conn.: Greenwood Press, 1970 (reprint of the original ed., London: George Routledge & Sons, Ltd., 1921).

Protestant Episcopal Church in the U.S.A. *The Hymnal 1940 Companion.* Prepared by the Joint Commission on the Revision of the Hymnal. 3rd rev. ed. New York: Church Pension Fund, 1956.

Poston, Elizabeth. *The Penguin Book of Christmas Carols.* London: Penguin Books, Ltd., 1965.

Routley, Erik. *The English Carol.* London: Herbert Jenkins, 1958.

Wheeler, Opal. *Sing for Christmas.* New York: E. P. Dutton, 1943.